Let Me
Introduce You
to
THE BIBLE

...so you can read it on your own

Advance Praise

"I am of the Jewish faith and I have worked in the legal profession all my life. I recently turned age 70 and I never have made any effort to study the Bible. I mentioned this to my friend Rob McKenzie, and Rob graciously offered to do readings and discussions of the Bible with me at some friendly lunches. Rob is a patient teacher and we had great discussions together. He greatly enhanced my understanding of the Bible. I feel very fortunate to have had the benefit of Rob's guidance and insight into the important subject of the Bible. I highly recommend this study as an important and meaningful experience."

— *Ken Brown*

"I have known Pastor Rob McKenzie for many years. His dedication and contribution to the work of the ministry have been a great example to all of us. In his book *Let Me Introduce You to the Bible* Pastor McKenzie has given us a wonderful tool to do what we all need most and that is to understand God's word. On the mission field of Mozambique there are very few books that give the help needed for the young and old in the Lord to get a handle on the big picture. Thank you, Rob, for this wonderful contribution."

— *Joel Troester, missionary to Mozambique*

"This practical book is a wonderful guide for anyone who has a serious interest in the Bible. The author, in a unique and interesting manner, provides an easily understood study of the layout of the scriptures as well as highlights key personalities within its pages. Those who are not familiar with the Bible will find it extremely helpful. The mature believer will also benefit by using this insightful work for evangelistic and general discipleship purposes. I heartily recommend this resource to you."

— *Paul Stevenson, D. Min.*

"I had the privilege to use Pastor McKenzie's Bible study with my father who knew little about the Bible. Throughout the study, my father asked many questions which led to opportunities to share the gospel ultimately leading him to a saving knowledge of Jesus Christ. Although the Bible study is primarily geared to providing people with an introduction the Bible, it also serves as a non-confrontational means of sharing the truth of God's word with them as well. I highly recommend it!"

— *Dr. Christian Barlow*

"In *Let Me Introduce You to the Bible*, Rob McKenzie provides a resource that will be a blessing to many, regardless of their level of familiarity with the Bible. For folks who are somewhat intimidated by the idea of Bible study, this excellent volume will alleviate their fears and welcome them into the wonder of discovery in God's timeless Word. The pedagogical approach will benefit novices and experienced readers alike — and lead them all through the fascinating story of scripture to encounter in a new and fresh way the person and work of Jesus Christ, Son of God, Savior of the world."

— *Sam Harbin, Chair of Bible & Theology, Lancaster Bible College*

Let Me Introduce You to

THE BIBLE

...so you can read it on your own

Robert J. McKenzie Jr.

Let Me Introduce You to THE BIBLE

to

...so you can read it on your own

Robert J. McKenzie Jr.
Muncy, Pennsylvania
rmck2@verizon.net

Let Me Introduce You to the Bible ... So You Can Read It on Your Own
Robert J. McKenzie Jr.
ISBN 978-0-578-75914-2 (pbk.)

Contents

Abbreviations

Scripture references in this book will use the following abreviations to cite the books of the Bible in the Old Testament and the New Testament.

Old Testament

Genesis	Gen.
Exodus	Ex.
Leviticus	Lev.
Numbers	Num.
Deuteronomy	Deut.
Joshua	Josh.
Judges	Judg.
Ruth	Ruth
1 & 2 Samuel	1&2 Sam.
1 & 2 Kings	1&2 Kgs.
1 & 2 Chronicles	1&2 Chron.
Ezra	Ezra
Nehemiah	Neh.
Esther	Esth.
Job	Job.
Psalms	Psa.
Proverbs	Prov.
Ecclesiastes	Eccl.
Song of Songs	Song.

Isaiah	Isa.
Jeremiah	Jer.
Lamentations	Lam.
Ezekiel	Exek.
Daniel	Dan.
Hosea	Hos.
Joel	Joel
Amos	Amos
Obadiah	Obad.
Jonah	Jonah
Micah	Mic.
Nahum	Nah.
Habakkuk	Hab.
Zephaniah	Zeph.
Haggai	Hag.
Zechariah	Zech.
Malachi	Mal.

New Testament

Matthew	Matt.
Mark	Mark
Luke	Luke
John	John
Acts	Acts
Romans	Rom.
1 & 2 Corinthians	1&2 Cor.
Galatians	Gal.
Ephesians	Eph.
Philippians	Phil.
Colossians	Col.

1 & 2 Thessalonians	1&2 Thes.
1 & 2 Timothy	1&2 Tim.
Titus	Titus
Philemon	Phile.
Hebrews	Heb.
James	James
1 & 2 Peter	1&2 Pet.
1, 2 & 3 John	1,2,3 Jn.
Jude	Jude
Revelation	Rev.

This book is dedicated to my church family,
whom I have had the privilege to serve
as your pastor these past 30 years.
Together we have grown in the grace and knowledge
of Jesus Christ.

This book is also dedicated to my wife Lynda,
your love,
and your partnership in life and ministry,
is an amazing blessing from God.

Preface

The book you are reading was written to help you become familiar with the greatest book ever written, the Bible, so that you can read the Bible with true understanding. You don't need a law degree to become acquainted with God's amazing book. The Bible is God's message to you. God wants you to be familiar with His sacred book because it reveals His plan for the world and His will for your life! For centuries, in every generation, people from all walks of life have found personal treasure from reading the Bible. There is a reason why the Bible is the best-selling book of all time and you will soon find out why!

Over the past twenty years I have shared the material included in this book with people of all ages and denominational backgrounds. Teens and adults, men and women, professionals and blue collar workers have been able to follow this plan and have benefited from this study. This study is not designed to promote a particular denomination or point of view. Rather, this study is designed for only one purpose, to introduce you to the Bible so you can read it on your own.

In this study we will divide the Bible into smaller sections. This will give us bite-sized portions to learn and enable us to see how the Bible fits together. The Bible can be divided into two main parts: the Old Testament and the New Testament. The Old Testament (also known as the Jewish Scriptures) contains all the writings before the time of Jesus Christ. The New Testament begins with the life and teaching of Jesus Christ. We will divide each of these major parts into smaller sections so that you can easily become familiar with all of the books of the Bible.

You can use this study with any Bible version. Keep in mind that the Old Testament was originally written in Hebrew, and the New Testament was written in Greek. Every Bible version is a translation of these ancient manuscripts and will say essentially the same thing. The difference in translations from version to version is minor. As you will discover, a comparison of Bible versions helps to shed light for better understanding of a passage in the Bible. I recommend that you find a Bible version that is easy to read and has print that is pleasant to your eye.

Together we will work on three outlines: two for the Old Testament and one for the New Testament. The first outline will cover the **Books of the Old Testament**. We will divide these into four sections: the Law, History, Poetry, and the Prophets. The second outline will cover the **People of the Old Testament**. This will follow the story line of the Old Testament and will also be divided into four sections: From Creation to the Flood, the Patriarchs, the Nation of Israel, and the Kingdom of Israel. The last outline will survey the **Books of the New Testament**. This last outline is divided into four sections: the Gospels, Acts, the

Epistles (Letters), and Revelation. Through the process of outlining these books you will come to understand their place in the Bible.

Each chapter will provide content for a section of the Bible, which will correspond to a section of the outline. You will be instructed on how to make your own outline, using the work sheets provided in each chapter. Each chapter will also include an assignment for reviewing the material which was already covered. There is also a reading assignment which is designed to give you a sampling of the various books and genres of the Bible. To receive the greatest benefit from your study it is best to complete the assigned worksheets before moving ahead to the next section. This will enable you to remember the material you have already completed in this study.

The writing of this book has been a labor of love and gratitude. I am so grateful to those who introduced me to the Bible and encouraged me to begin reading it over 40 years ago. Reading the Bible and talking about what it says with others is something I love to do. God's word has had a powerful effect on my life. And it has been a great blessing to see what happens in other's lives once they begin to read the Bible. In fact, a study of history will show that everywhere the Bible has traveled it has brought freedom and life to those who received it.

Over the past twenty years I have shared the material included in this book with people of all ages and denominational backgrounds. . . . this study is designed for only one purpose, to introduce you to the Bible so you can read it on your own.

The publishing of this book would not have been possible without the assistance of friends who believed that this project was a worthy cause. I want to especially recognize Tina Steinbacher for her patience and expertise in the original setup of the outlines in this book, and Rod Dewald, for his grasp of grammar and his insightful suggestions. And I am also grateful to Fred Walters for guiding this book to publication. Fred, from the first conversation we had about this book I heard you express what I hoped could be accomplished. Your generous time and help has made this possible.

It is my hope that once you have become familiar with the Bible and begin reading it on your own, that you will want to introduce this treasure to others! Next, you will find some suggestions on how to use this book to help others.

Rob McKenzie

How to Use this Book to Help Others

In addition to helping you to become familiar with the Bible, this book has another purpose. The secondary purpose is for you to use this book to help others to become familiar with the Bible. Just as you will be guided through the material laid out in this book, you will find that you too can guide others through this same material. You will be amazed at how much more you will learn when you make the step from learner to teacher.

Leading a Bible Study with Others

This study is useful in both one-on-one settings and for leading group Bible studies; it can be used in the informal setting of a home or the more formal setting of a classroom in a church. Let me give you some examples of how this book has successfully helped to introduce the Bible to many people in a variety of settings.

Parents have used this study with their teen sons and daughters. Adult children have enjoyed doing this study with their elderly parents. Because there are twelve chapters, this study fits well in a **Sunday School** class quarter (13 weeks). Review questions are supplied in the appendix for a review lesson as well. **Small groups** for adults in a church, or cell groups for teens within a church's Youth Group, all can benefit from this study.

Another exciting opportunity for using this study has been with **neighbors and acquaintances**. Both **church-attenders and non-church-attenders** have found this study helpful and interesting. Many people have not yet been introduced to the Bible in a helpful way; some of these are often interested in learning more about the Bible when someone they know can introduce them to it in a non-threatening way. People from many different denominations and faiths have found this study to be interesting and helpful. All it takes is an invitation.

The way in which I initiate Bible studies is to ask an acquaintance or friend if he has ever read the Bible. Some people have, but many have never read God's book. Even people who consider themselves to be religious are not always familiar with the Bible. To people who are interested I explain that I have a study that can familiarize them with the whole Bible in a short time. I let them know that I would be willing to get together with them privately to do the study together.

(I have met in homes, libraries, and restaurants.) Then I ask them, "Would you be interested?"

If you ever have the experience of introducing someone to God's word, you will find it is a very satisfying one. I have often observed that once a person begins to read and understand the Bible, it reveals an area of his or her life that they did not know exists! When you introduce someone to the Bible, you may find that you are introducing them to God.

When you introduce someone to the Bible, you may find that you are introducing them to God.

Missionaries who serve overseas can adapt this study into the languages of the people to whom they are ministering. The outlines that are employed in this book can be translated by the missionaries into French, Spanish, Arabic, or any other language. The Bible is being translated in every language of mankind, and people in every nation are hungering for God's truth. But until people become familiar with the Bible, God's word will remain bread that is out of reach. But imagine what could happen when ordinary people have access to a simple tool like this study so that they can become familiar with the Bible? And then imagine the confidence they will have when they are able to introduce God's word to their families and friends.

Planting the Seed of God's Word in the Hearts of Others

Jesus told a parable about a man who was scattering seed (Matt. 13:3-9,18-23). The seed landed on soil with various conditions: hard soil, shallow soil, soil with thorns, and good soil. The condition of the soil determined whether or not the seed produced fruit. Jesus concluded by exhorting everyone to truly hear what He was saying. He then explained that the seed in the story represents the word of God and the soil represents the hearts of people.

This parable has made an impression on me in three ways:

Regarding the seed; just as a grain of wheat has the power to produce new life, the word of God has supernatural power to bring about spiritual life in the heart of anyone who truly understands and believes. This is why Jesus also said that man shall not live by bread alone, but by every word that comes from the mouth of God (Matt. 4:4). This study is designed to help you to become familiar with the Bible so that you can read it with understanding. When God's word is understood and believed, the result is spiritual fruit in the heart of that person, which other people will see. As you grow in your understanding of the Bible, so will your faith grow.

Regarding the sower; to plant the seed in the soil, someone needs to scatter it. If you have benefited from being able to read and understand the Bible then most likely you want others to share the joy and peace that you now experience. It is my hope that this book gives you a framework with which you can help others become familiar with God's word. If you have the opportunity to share this study with someone you know, then you will see the power of God's word at work in the heart of your friend.

Regarding the soil; the condition of the soil determines whether or not the seed produces fruit. Similarly, the word of God does not have the same effect on all people. Not everyone is interested in hearing what God has to say. But some will be interested. You won't know who will be interested until you give them an opportunity to become familiar with God's amazing book. May God guide you and use you in his blessed work.

Part 1
Old Testament Books

Old Testament Books

The Christian Bible is divided into two main parts: the Old Testament and the New Testament. The New Testament begins with events related to Jesus Christ. The Old Testament consists of all of the books of the Bible written before the coming of Jesus. Many people of the Jewish faith do not recognize Jesus as the Messiah or Christ (Messiah means anointed one in Hebrew; Christ means anointed one in Greek). For this reason the Jewish Scriptures only include the books of the Old Testament.

In this section you will be making your own **personal outline** for all of the books of the Old Testament! When you are finished your outline will look like the figure on the next page. Your outline will show the division of the Old Testament books into four sections. The chapters that follow give you information about each of the books in that section and will explain why these books were grouped together. Each chapter will provide a model for the outline you are working on. Examples are given in each chapter to guide you in the making of your own outline. Directions for writing your outline will be located in a box. The portion for you to write will be in **bold print and underlined**.

The next four chapters will give you information for the biblical books which correspond to each of the four sections of your outline: the Law, the History Books, the Poetry Books, and the Prophets. You are now ready to begin with the Law.

Old Testament Books

I. Law = 5 Books

Genesis = Beginnings
Creation, Fall, Flood, Promised Land,
Sodom & Gomorrah

Exodus = Way Out
10 Plagues, Red Sea,
10 Commandments, Tabernacle

Leviticus = Levi
Priests, sacrifices, Levites

Numbers = Counted
People numbered (2 million)
40 yrs in wilderness

Deuteronomy = 2nd Time
Moses' farewell sermons

II. History = 12 Books

Joshua = he led Israel into the
Promised Land.
Judges = Israel's leaders before
they had kings.
Ruth = she became David's great-
grandmother.

1&2 Samuel = the life of David
(from shepherd boy to king)
1&2 Kings = the history of Israel's
kings after David
(Civil War = North vs. South)
1&2 Chronicles = Records
(Chronicles) of the southern
kings (Judah)

Ezra = the temple in Jerusalem was
rebuilt after captivity
Nehemiah = the walls of Jerusalem
were rebuilt after captivity
Esther = how an orphaned Jewish
girl became Queen of Persia

III. Poetry = 5 Books

Job = A good man's faith
perseveres thru very bad times.

Psalms = Prayers & songs of praise
(mostly by David)

Proverbs = Wise sayings on how to
live wisely (by Solomon)

Ecclesiastes = A man's search for
satisfaction (by Solomon)

Song of Songs = A song about
marriage love (by Solomon)

IV. Prophets = 17 Books

A. <u>Major Prophets</u> = 5 Books
Isaiah (66)
Jeremiah (52)
Lamentations (5)
Ezekiel (48)
Daniel (12)

B. <u>Minor Prophets</u> = 12 Books

Hosea	Joel
Amos	Obadiah
Jonah	Micah
Nahum	Habakkuk
Zephaniah	Haggai
Zechariah	Malachi

CHAPTER 1

The Law (Torah)

I n this chapter you will become familiar with the first five books of the Old Testament, which are referred to as "the Law." The Jewish Scriptures refer to this section as the "Torah," which can be translated as "law" or "instruction." Each of these biblical books contains God's commands and instructions, some more than others. However, you will also find in these books the account of God's intervention in human history. Biblical history is truly His-story, or a telling of the events in the outworking of God's plan. God's plan includes the creation of the world, and the calling and redeeming of His covenant people. History began with the creation of the earth and the universe, with man being the pinnacle of God's creative work. God's work of providence, in which He orchestrates His redemptive plan, will continue until the end of time. In the law you will see God's holiness, sovereignty, and mercy displayed in His conversations, judgments, and covenants.

Redemption: God's work of setting sinners free from the power of sin and death.

It is believed that Moses was the author of these five books. He was a witness to most of the events recorded in this section. Those events that Moses did not witness were revealed to him when God spoke to Moses face to face on Mt. Sinai (Ex. 33:11).

Sovereignty: God being in control of all things; God ruling over creation.

Instructions for Your Outline

When you turn this page you will find two outlines facing each other. The outline on the left is the model; the outline on the right is your outline. Below are instructions for writing your outline, followed by more information to familiarize you with this part of the Bible.

> Write **Law** in the top left section of your outline, next to Roman numeral one. Next to "Law" put an **equal sign** (=), followed by **5 Books**.

Old Testament Books

I. *Law = 5 Books*

    Genesis = Beginnings
      Creation, Fall, Flood, Promised Land,
      Sodom & Gomorrah

    Exodus = Way Out
      10 Plagues, Red Sea,
      10 Commandments, Tabernacle

    Leviticus = Levi
      Priests, sacrifices, Levites

    Numbers = Counted
      People numbered (2 million)
      40 yrs in wilderness

    Deuteronomy = 2nd Time
      Moses' farewell sermons

II.

III.

IV.

Old Testament Books

I.

II.

III.

IV.

Genesis

Genesis
= Beginnings

It is in the first book of the Bible, Genesis, where the account of **creation** is found (Gen. 1). Genesis gets its name because it tells us how the universe was "birthed" by God.

The key word for you to associate with Genesis is **"Beginnings."** The **Fall** refers to the sin of the first man and woman, Adam & Eve. God placed them in a garden paradise. He gave them fruit from several different types of fruit trees to eat. God's only command for them was not to eat fruit from one tree; the tree of the knowledge of good and evil. When Adam and Eve sinned, they lost (or fell from) their holy standing with God. Every person born since Adam sinned is born with a sin nature. This means that selfishness and resisting God's will is a part of our human nature. You will read about these events in your reading assignment (Gen. 3).

Genesis also tells us about the worldwide **flood** that happened during the time of Noah (Gen. 7). The flood was God's judgment for sin. All living things that lived on dry land died in the flood, except for Noah, his family, and the animals on the ark. Fossils that are found in our modern day provide evidence of this ancient judgment of God.

Another event recorded in Genesis is the covenant of God to Abraham and his descendants concerning the **Promised Land** (Gen. 12). Abraham is the father of the nation of Israel. God made a covenant with Abraham that included the promise of land, descendants, and through him a great blessing to all the people of the world.

Also included in the Book of Genesis is the judgment of **Sodom and Gomorrah** (Gen. 19). The cities of Sodom and Gomorrah were destroyed by fire and brimstone from God as judgment for their wickedness.

Exodus

The word **Exodus** is from the Greek word which means **"a way out."** We get our word "exit" from the same etymological root. Exodus records the beginning of the Nation of Israel. This started with their deliverance from slavery when God made a way out of Egypt. In time you will read about the **10 plagues** which God brought upon the Egyptians to convince their king, Pharaoh, to let the Israelites go

(Ex. 7-11). God brought the Israelites out of Egypt by separating the water of the **Red Sea** so that the Israelites walked through the sea on a seabed of dry ground (Ex. 14).

Moses led the people to Mt. Sinai where God gave the Israelites the **Ten Commandments**. Your reading assignment will help you remember where to locate the Ten Commandments in the Bible (Ex. 20). In addition to the Ten Commandments (moral law), God also gave Moses all the laws to guide the Israelites in their civil government and ceremonial worship of God; including instructions for a portable temple (**Tabernacle**) which they would build to worship God (Ex. 25-27). Inside the courtyard of the Tabernacle was an altar on which the priests offered sacrifices to atone for the sins of the people.

Exodus
= Way Out

Leviticus

> On the next line of your outline write the name of the third book, **Leviticus**, followed by an **equal sign**, and **Levi**. Underneath Leviticus write the following words: **Priests, sacrifices, Levites**.

So that you can better understand the significance of this book it will be helpful to look at the family tree in the Appendix, titled **Abraham to Aaron Family Tree**. When God appeared to Moses at the burning bush, He referred to Himself as the God of <u>Abraham</u>, the God of <u>Isaac</u> (Abraham's son), and the God of <u>Jacob</u> (Isaac's son). These are the Patriarchs of the Israelites.

The Israelites get their name from Jacob, whose name God changed to Israel. Jacob had twelve sons, who became the fathers of the twelve tribes of Israel. The tribe of **Levi** consisted of the descendants of Jacob's third son. Moses was from the tribe of Levi. God chose Moses' brother Aaron to be the first priest among the Israelites. The priesthood was not open to everyone. Only Aaron, his sons, and their descendants were chosen to serve as **priests**. Only priests were allowed to offer **sacrifices** to God on behalf of the people. The rest of the tribe of Levi were called the **Levites**. Only Levites were chosen to assist the priests in their religious duties. Jesus' parable of the Good Samaritan in the New Testament makes mention of a priest and a Levite (Luke 10:29-37).

Leviticus
= Levi

The book of **Leviticus** means "pertaining to the Levites." In this book God instructed the Israelites in His many laws about sacrifices, the means of becoming ceremonially clean, kosher foods, the religious feasts, and the behavior of the priests. The priests and Levites were responsible for observing God's law and teaching it to the people.

Numbers

On the next line of your outline write the name of the fourth book, **Numbers**, followed by an **equal sign**, and **Counted**. Underneath Numbers write the following words: **people numbered (2 million)**. And below that you can also write: **40 yrs. in wilderness**.

Numbers = Counted

Before the Israelites departed from Mt. Sinai for the Promised Land, a census was taken that **counted** all the men of Israel who were 20 years of age and older. This is the meaning behind the name of the book of **Numbers** (to number = to count). The census found over 600,000 men who could be counted on to fight in war. With this number we can estimate the number of Israelites who came out of slavery in Egypt. Add a woman for every man 20 years and older. The number of adults comes to 1,200,000. Then add an approximate number of children under 20 years (~800,000). The sum of the number of adults and children comes to **two million**. God brought two million Israelites out of Egypt and cared for them during their forty year journey to the Promised Land.

Even though the Israelites saw, with their own eyes, God's faithfulness to them, they still complained about the difficulties of their journey, which God used to test their faith. When the Israelites rebelled against Moses' leadership and threatened to return to Egypt, God punished them by **extending their journey through the wilderness for forty years**. It was only after the older generation, who were over twenty years old at the time of the census, died in the wilderness that God led them into the Promised Land. Numbers records some of the events that occurred during the forty years of the Israelites wandering in the wilderness.

Deuteronomy

The fifth and last book in this section is Deuteronomy.

Deuteronomy = 2nd Time

Write **Deuteronomy** followed by an **equal sign** and **2nd time**. Underneath Deuteronomy write the following words: **Moses' farewell sermons**.

After 40 years of wandering in the desert, Moses led the Israelites to the border of the Promised Land. He was 80 years old at the time of the Exodus, but he was now 120 years old. God told Moses that he would not lead the people into the Promised Land, and that he would soon die. Moses then gathered the Israelites together to remind them of what God did for them and what God commanded them to do. The name **Deuteronomy** means "second law," but it is really a **second time** that the same law was being rehearsed. The older generation had died in the wilderness and the younger generation needed to be reminded of God's faithfulness and of God's laws, so that they would live for God in the land He was giving them. In these **final sermons**, Moses reminds the people of Israel's history up to this point and repeats

God's laws. The two books where you will find the Ten Commandments are Exodus 20 and Deuteronomy 5.

Instructions for Review

The purpose of the following exercises is to reinforce the information you have just learned. This will help you to remember and use what you have studied and learned. It will help if you say the names of the books out loud as you do each of the exercises. The first exercise contains lists of the five books we have covered with open spaces for you to fill in the name of the missing book. It is important that you remember the names of the books and their proper order. In the second exercise you will put the books in their proper order, while saying the names out loud (i.e. #1 Genesis, #2 Exodus…). In the third exercise you will match the theme of each book of the Bible by matching the letter next to each theme with the correct Bible book. As you complete each exercise speak it out loud so that you will easily remember what you have learned.

Old Testament Review
The Law — the First 5 books

1. Fill in what is missing:

#1	#2	#3	#4	#5
Genesis	_____	_____	Genesis	Genesis
_____	Exodus	_____	Exodus	_____
Leviticus	_____	_____	_____	_____
_____	Numbers	Numbers	_____	_____
Deuteronomy	_____	Deuteronomy	_____	_____

2. Put each column in the proper order: (assign numbers 1-5)

#1	#2	#3
_____ Leviticus	_____ Genesis	_____ Numbers
_____ Genesis	_____ Numbers	_____ Deuteronomy
_____ Deuteronomy	_____ Leviticus	_____ Exodus
_____ Numbers	_____ Exodus	_____ Leviticus
_____ Exodus	_____ Deuteronomy	_____ Genesis

3. Match the theme with the book of the Bible:

A. Genesis   _____ You need to hear this again (a second time)

B. Exodus   _____ What about Levi?

C. Leviticus   _____ You can count me in!

D. Numbers   _____ There is a way out!

E. Deuteronomy   _____ Let's start at the very beginning.

Reading Assignment

Now it is time to sample the Scriptures which we have studied. Your reading assignment is nine chapters: chapters 1-7 of Genesis, and chapters 19 and 20 of Exodus.

Genesis 1-7
Exodus 19-20

Here is a preview of what you will be reading.

The **first seven chapters of Genesis** present the biblical record of prehistoric times. In **Genesis 1** you will read how God created the earth and the universe. Even though He could have done so by His power with the snap of His fingers, He chose to create all things in six days. God ceased from His creative work on the seventh day, which is the basis for a Sabbath, or day of rest for man, and for a seven day week. You will notice that man and animals were created on the same day. A literal reading of these chapters suggests that dinosaurs and man lived on the earth at the same time, having been created on the same day.

In **Genesis 2** God's creation of man is expanded on to give the details of the way God made man in His image, both male and female. The basis for the institution of marriage is presented in this chapter in the relationship of Adam and Eve. **Genesis 3** reveals how death is the consequence of sin caused by Adam and Eve's disobedience of God's command. Through Adam's sin, death and disease came into the world. Also, the evidence of a "sin nature" which was passed on to Adam's descendants is found in Cain's murder of his brother Abel in **Genesis 4**.

In **Genesis 5** you will discover that the average life span for people who lived before the flood was around 900 years! This chapter tells of the lineage between Adam and Noah and reveals to us that the flood occurred around 1600 years after God created Adam. **Genesis 6-7** introduces you to Noah and to the details of the worldwide flood.

The subject of **dinosaurs** is interesting to many people, especially as to how they fit in the biblical record. The common belief among those who reject the literal teaching of the Bible is that the world is billions of years old and that dinosaurs preceded man by millions of years. But is this view necessary? The reality of dinosaurs does not contradict the Bible. Creation scientists theorize that dinosaurs were created at the same time as man, and therefore dinosaurs were on the ark with Noah. These scientists support their theories with these points. The largest dinosaurs came from eggs no larger than a football. It was not necessary for Noah to have full grown dinosaurs on the ark. Dragon legends are found in ancient literature from around the world; and so are tales of a flood. A dragon was what these creatures were called before the word dinosaur was coined in the 1800s. The Bible even has a description of what appears to be dinosaurs in the ancient book of Job (See Job 40:15-24;

The reality of dinosaurs does not contradict the Bible. The flood provides the best explanation for the thousands of fossils that have been discovered.

41:1-10). The flood provides the best explanation for the thousands of fossils that have been discovered. The internet has many websites that examine creation science. One that I recommend is "Answers in Genesis."

In **Exodus 19-20**, you will read about the giving of the Ten Commandments to Moses and the Israelites at Mt. Sinai. God engraved these commands on two stone tablets. Before God put these commands into writing, our human understanding of righteousness and justice came from our conscience, the result of being created in God's image. However, the sinfulness of our hearts (because of our sin nature) blinds us to the truth on our own. God's law teaches us the righteousness of God's character and establishes the universal standard of morality. Consider this: apart from the existence of God and His law, it is impossible to come up with a consistent basis for morality for society, which is why it is good to know these commandments and where they are located in the Bible.

To complete this reading assignment read a chapter a day, or read it all in one or two sittings; it's up to you to decide the pace. But it will benefit you to finish reading these chapters before continuing work on your outline. Completing each reading assignment will reinforce the location of each book, and will familiarize you with the content in this section of the Bible.

Earlier in this chapter a reference was made to the parable of the Good Samaritan with the Scripture location cited (Luke 10:29-37). This is the way verses are indicated – Book, chapter, the starting verse followed by the ending verse.

When you have completed your assignments, we will continue with the next section of the Old Testament: the History Books.

CHAPTER 2

The History Books

In this chapter we will learn about the next twelve books of the Old Testament, the History Books. These books record the history of the nation of Israel in the Promised Land after the time of Moses. They are written in a style that is interesting and insightful in revealing the people and customs of that time. The Bible records Israel's history because it reveals God's relationship with His chosen people. Anyone who reads these books will learn much about God's character and God's ways through His actions towards the people of Israel, with whom He had made a covenant to be their God. That makes these books more than history, these books teach theology.

Instructions For Your Outline

When you turn this page you will find two outlines facing each other. The outline on the left is the model; the outline on the right is your outline. You will find this same format in every chapter. Below are instructions for writing your outline, followed by the information that will familiarize you with the History books.

We will group the History books into three clusters of books, leaving a space between each cluster. This will give visual clarity and will aid your memory.

Write **History** to the right side of Roman numeral two (II). Next to History Books write an **equal sign** (=), followed by **12 Books**.

The figure on the page facing your outline is your guide in making your outline.

Old Testament Books

I. Law = 5 Books

Genesis = Beginnings
  Creation, Fall, Flood, Promised Land,
  Sodom & Gomorrah

Exodus = Way Out
  10 Plagues, Red Sea,
  10 Commandments, Tabernacle

Leviticus = Levi
  Priests, sacrifices, Levites

Numbers = Counted
  People numbered (2 million)
  40 yrs in wilderness

Deuteronomy = 2nd Time
  Moses' farewell sermons

II. History = 12 Books

Joshua = he led Israel into the
  Promised Land.
Judges = Israel's leaders before
  they had kings.
Ruth = she became David's great-
  grandmother.

1&2 Samuel = the life of David
  (from shepherd boy to king)
1&2 Kings = the history of Israel's
  kings after David
  (Civil War = North vs. South)
1&2 Chronicles = Records
  (Chronicles) of the southern
  kings (Judah)

Ezra = the temple in Jerusalem was
  rebuilt after captivity
Nehemiah = the walls of Jerusalem
  were rebuilt after captivity
Esther = how an orphaned Jewish
  girl became Queen of Persia

III.

IV.

Old Testament Books

I. *Law = 5 Books*

    Genesis = Beginnings
       Creation, Fall, Flood, Promised Land,
       Sodom & Gomorrah

    Exodus = Way Out
       10 Plagues, Red Sea,
       10 Commandments, Tabernacle

    Leviticus = Levi
       Priests, sacrifices, Levites

    Numbers = Counted
       People numbered (2 million)
       40 yrs in wilderness

    Deuteronomy = 2nd Time
       Moses' farewell sermons

II.

III.

IV.

Joshua, Judges, Ruth

> We will begin the first cluster of books by writing **Joshua**, followed by an **equal sign**, and **he led Israel into Promised Land**. Under Joshua on the next line write **Judges**, followed by an **equal sign**, and **Israel's leaders before they had kings**. The next book under Judges is **Ruth**, followed by an **equal sign** and **she became David's great-grandmother**.

The Bible records Israel's history because it reveals God's relationship with His chosen people.

This first cluster of three books tells the story of Israel's early history in the Promised Land. The book of **Joshua** records **how he led the Israelites in conquering** the land which God promised to them. Joshua was chosen by God to lead the nation of Israel into the Promised Land after the death of Moses. The land was filled with the people of other nations who had to be conquered. After the major battles were won under Joshua's leadership, the Promised Land was divided and each of the twelve tribes of Israel was given territory.

If you have difficulty in understanding how war is acceptable to God, you can read Deuteronomy 18:9-12 to learn about the wickedness of these people who were deserving of God's judgment.

The book of **Judges** continues Israel's history after Joshua died. After they were living in the Promised Land God's people turned their backs on Him, they broke their covenant with God so God removed His protection from them. When other nations brutally oppressed them, they cried out to God for deliverance. In response to their prayers God raised up **"judges"** who **led Israel to victory** by removing the foreign armies from the land. This cycle of sin-oppression-repentance-deliverance is repeated often during this time in Israel's history because the people "did what was right in their own eyes," instead of following the Law which God had given them. The book of **Ruth** tells the story of a family who lived during the time of the Judges. This short narrative tells the love story of a widow who remarries and becomes the **great-grandmother of David**. David became the most famous king of Israel.

Samuel, Kings, Chronicles

The second cluster of books actually has six books.

> **Leave a space** between the first cluster of three and this cluster of books. First and Second Samuel is written as **1&2 Samuel**, followed by an **equal sign**, and **the life of David (from shepherd boy to king)**. The next pair of books is First and Second Kings, written as **1&2 Kings**, followed by an **equal sign**, and **the history of Israel's kings after David (Civil War = North vs. South)**.

You will probably need an extra line to get all of this information on your outline. When you do, write so that the names of the books stand out.

> Now write the last pair of books in this cluster as **1&2 Chronicles**, followed by an **equal sign** (=) and **Records (Chronicles) of the southern kings (Judah)**. Use the figure in this chapter to guide you.

This cluster of books follows Israel's history from the time of the judges through the reigns of Israel's kings. The rule of Israel's kings ended when the Babylonians destroyed the city of Jerusalem and its temple, and took the survivors away into captivity in Babylon. The first pair of books, **1&2 Samuel** gets their name from a man named Samuel who was a prophet and a priest and a judge. Samuel anointed David as king of Israel. These two books include events in **David's life**, beginning when **he was a shepherd boy**, who killed a giant with a slingshot. This narrative of David's life also covers his reign as Israel's greatest king. God promised David that the Messiah would be a descendant of his (2 Sam. 7:12-13).

The second pair of books, **1&2 Kings** tells the **history of Israel's kings after David's reign**. Israel's history was interrupted by a **Civil War** which pitted the ten northern tribes against the two southern tribes of Israel. This resulted in fracturing the nation into two kingdoms: the **north** retained the name <u>Israel</u>; the **south** took the name of the prominent tribe of <u>Judah</u>. A reading of 1&2 Kings will find major events in the reigns of the northern kings of Israel and the southern kings of Judah.

The last pair of books, **1&2 Chronicles** tells the **history of the southern kings of Judah**. A chronicle is a **record**, and only the reigns of the kings of Judah are recorded in this book because David was from the tribe of Judah. His line of descendants is important because of God's promise concerning the Messiah. The Messiah would be called "the son of David."

Anyone who reads these books will learn much about God's character and God's ways through His actions towards the people of Israel, with whom He had made a covenant to be their God. That makes these books more than history; these books teach theology.

Ezra, Nehemiah, Esther

> <u>Leave a space</u> between the middle cluster of books with this final cluster in this section. Write <u>Ezra</u>, followed by an **equal sign** and **the temple in Jerusalem was rebuilt after captivity**. Underneath write **Nehemiah**, followed by an **equal sign** and **the walls of Jerusalem were rebuilt after captivity**. And finally write <u>Esther</u>, followed by an **equal sign** and **how an orphaned Jewish girl became Queen of Persia**.

The time period in Israel's history for this last cluster of books is after the captivity. As mentioned above, the Babylonian army destroyed the city of Jerusalem, which was the capital city where the temple was located. The temple was at the center of Jewish religion and worship. The survivors of the kingdom of Judah were carried away into Babylon, where they were allowed to keep their customs. The captivity ended after 70 years when the Persians conquered the Babylonians and granted the "Jews" (from Judah) permission to return to their homeland. The book of **Ezra** tells **how the temple was rebuilt** by the Jews who returned from captivity. This book takes its name from Ezra, a priest who taught the people God's law and encouraged them to live in obedience to His law. **Nehemiah** lived during the same time period as Ezra. Under his leadership **the walls of Jerusalem were rebuilt**. In ancient times a city without walls was defenseless.

Both Ezra and Nehemiah describe what life was like for Jews who returned to the land of Israel after the Babylonian Captivity. But not all of the Jews returned. The book of **Esther** shows how God even watched over those Jews who decided to live in Persia. Esther was an **orphaned Jewish girl** who lived in Persia. She was raised by her cousin after her parents died. Esther became **queen of Persia** when Xerxes was king. She was used by God to stop the extermination of the Jewish people.

Instructions for Review

The following exercises will both reinforce and help you to remember what you have learned. Speak each of the names of the books as you complete these exercises. In the first exercise there are five lists of the twelve books we have covered, with open spaces for you to fill in the name of the missing book. Start at the top of each list and say the name of the book as you go down the list, filling in the open spaces in each list. The second exercise requires you to match the book of the Bible with the appropriate theme by writing the correct letter in the blank. You will find that the clusters of books have been kept separate to help you to easily remember them. Each exercise should be spoken out loud as you complete it.

Old Testament Review

The History Books: Joshua – Esther (12 books)

1. Fill in what is missing:

#1	#2	#3	#4	#5
Joshua	*Joshua*	Joshua	Joshua	Joshua
Judges	*Judges*	Judges	Judges	*Judges*
Ruth	*Ruth*	Ruth	Ruth	*Ruth*
1 Samuel	1 Samuel	*1 Samuel*	1 Samuel	*1 Samuel*
2 Samuel	2 Samuel	*2 Samuel*	2 Samuel	*2 Samuel*
1 Kings	1 Kings	*1 Kings*	1 Kings	*1 Kings*
2 Kings	2 Kings	*2 Kings*	2 Kings	*2 Kings*
1 Chronicles	1 Chronicles	*1 Chronicles*	1 Chronicles	*1 Chronicles*
2 Chronicles	2 Chronicles	*2 Chronicles*	2 Chronicles	*2 Chronicles*
Ezra	Ezra	Ezra	*Ezra*	*Ezra*
Nehemiah	Nehemiah	Nehemiah	*Nehemiah*	*Nehemiah*
Esther	Esther	Esther	*Esther*	*Esther*

2. Match the book of the Bible with the appropriate theme:

_B_ Joshua   A. She was David's great-grandmother.

_C_ Judges   B. He led them into the Promised land after Moses died.

_A_ Ruth   C. Israel's leaders before they had kings.

_D_ 1 & 2 Samuel   D. The life of David: from shepherd boy to king.

_E_ 1 & 2 Kings   E. The history of Israel's kings after David (civil war).

_F_ 1 & 2 Chronicles   F. Records (chronicles) of just the southern kings (Judah).

_I_ Ezra   G. How an orphaned Jewish girl became queen of Persia.

_H_ Nehemiah   H. The walls of Jerusalem were rebuilt, after captivity.

_G_ Esther   I. The Temple in Jerusalem was rebuilt, after captivity.

Reading Assignment

Now it is time to sample the Scriptures which we have studied. Your reading assignment is eight chapters including selections from the books of Joshua, Judges, Ruth and 1 Samuel.

Joshua 1-3
Judges 6-7, 13-14
Ruth 1-4
1 Samuel 16-18

Here is a Preview of What You will be Reading

Joshua 1-3: In Joshua 1 Joshua takes over the leadership of Israel after Moses died. Moses left some big shoes to fill, but God promised to be with Joshua in the same way He had been with Moses. Moses is often referred to as God's servant. In Joshua 2 you will meet a prostitute named Rahab: a condemned woman in the condemned city of Jericho. But her faith in the God of Israel was clearly demonstrated and was graciously rewarded. Then, in Joshua 3 you will read of the trust in God that was needed when Israel crossed into the Promised Land, which was already inhabited by other nations. The crossing of the Jordan River into the Promised Land and the Israelites crossing of the Red Sea to escape Egyptian slavery are nearly identical miracles. Both miraculous were done by the power of God. And both miracles allowed the Israelites to cross through on dry ground!

Judges 6-7, 13-14: In Judges 6-7 you will be introduced to Gideon, one of Israel's judges. Gideon led the Israelites to victory over a nation that oppressed them. Through Gideon God showed that victory depended not on the power of a human army, but on the presence of the almighty God! In Judges 13-14 you will read about Samson, the strongest man who ever lived…that is until his hair was cut! Samson did great feats of strength by the power of God. However, he had weaknesses that caused bad situations that ended with sad consequences. In the end, his faith was rewarded and he found mercy with God.

Ruth 1-4: The book of Ruth will give you a glimpse of the faith of God-fearing people who lived during the time of the judges. Ruth was a foreigner who married into the Jewish nation. Her faith and life story are proof that God is a "personal God" who accepts and honors anyone who trusts in Him. Ruth became the great-grandmother of King David.

1 Samuel 16-18: You will certainly enjoy reading these chapters from 1 Samuel. David is introduced in 1 Samuel 16 as the one chosen to be the next king of Israel. Being anointed with oil by God's prophet Samuel was symbolic of God's choice. The designation of being "the anointed one" (or "Messiah") was accompanied by the presence of the Holy Spirit. The presence of the Holy Spirit became apparent in David's faith when he fought the giant Goliath in 1 Samuel 17. Saul, the reigning king of

Israel, saw God's blessing of David and he was filled with jealousy and became afraid that David would replace him. In 1 Samuel 18 you will read of Saul's initial attempts to kill David. This caused David to live on the run as a refugee for several years.

You can read a chapter a day or read it all in two or three sittings; it's up to you to decide the pace. But it will benefit you to finish reading these chapters before continuing on to the next part of your outline. Completing each reading assignment will help you to remember the location and content of each book in this section of the Bible.

When you have completed your assignments, we will pick up with the next section of the Old Testament: the Poetry Books.

CHAPTER 3

The Poetry Books

In this chapter we will discuss the five Poetry Books of the Old Testament. Hebrew poetry has two distinctive characteristics which you will find in the five books of this section. One characteristic is the use of parallelism, in which a sentence or phrase is paired with another sentence or phrase. The second line will provide either a complementary thought or a contrasting thought. When read together both lines give a clearer picture of the author's point. Another characteristic is the use of figurative language and word pictures, which are more capable of conveying emotion than simple descriptive statements. By way of example, here are the first two verses of Psalm 23:

> 1   *The LORD is my shepherd;*
> *I shall not want.*
> 2   *He makes me to lie down in green pastures;*
> *He leads me beside still waters.*

The author describes God as a shepherd and himself as a lamb who trusts his shepherd, which is a comforting word picture. In verse 1, the two lines are complementary: the author (David) knows that he doesn't have to worry about his needs because God is like a shepherd to him. Verse 2 provides two lines that are similar to emphasize the point he is making, which is to explain his trust: green pastures and calm waters are comforting and nurturing for a sheep. Hebrew poetry is both pleasant to hear and easy to remember.

The Poetry Books are also wisdom literature because of the topics addressed in these writings. The book of Job addresses the issue of suffering. The book of Psalms reflects worship by one who is confident in the sovereignty of God. The book of Proverbs gives instruction on how to become wise in living. The book of Ecclesiastes wrestles with the subjects of satisfaction and fulfillment. And Song of Songs is about the love between a man and his wife.

Old Testament Books

I. Law = 5 Books

Genesis = Beginnings
  Creation, Fall, Flood, Promised Land,
  Sodom & Gomorrah

Exodus = Way Out
  10 Plagues, Red Sea,
  10 Commandments, Tabernacle

Leviticus = Levi
  Priests, sacrifices, Levites

Numbers = Counted
  People numbered (2 million)
  40 yrs in wilderness

Deuteronomy = 2nd Time
  Moses' farewell sermons

II. History = 12 Books

Joshua = he led Israel into the
  Promised Land.
Judges = Israel's leaders before
  they had kings.
Ruth = she became David's great-
  grandmother.

1&2 Samuel = the life of David
  (from shepherd boy to king)
1&2 Kings = the history of Israel's
  kings after David
  (Civil War = North vs. South)
1&2 Chronicles = Records
  (Chronicles) of the southern
  kings (Judah)

Ezra = the temple in Jerusalem was
  rebuilt after captivity
Nehemiah = the walls of Jerusalem
  were rebuilt after captivity
Esther = how an orphaned Jewish
  girl became Queen of Persia

III. Poetry = 5 Books

Job = A good man's faith
  perseveres thru very bad times.

Psalms = Prayers & songs of praise
(mostly by David)

Proverbs = Wise sayings on how to
  live wisely (by Solomon)

Ecclesiastes = A man's search for
  satisfaction (by Solomon)

Song of Songs = A song about
  marriage love (by Solomon)

IV.

Old Testament Books

I. Law = 5 Books

Genesis = Beginnings
Creation, Fall, Flood, Promised Land,
Sodom & Gomorrah

Exodus = Way Out
10 Plagues, Red Sea,
10 Commandments, Tabernacle

Leviticus = Levi
Priests, sacrifices, Levites

Numbers = Counted
People numbered (2 million)
40 yrs in wilderness

Deuteronomy = 2nd Time
Moses' farewell sermons

II. History = 12 Books

Joshua = he led Israel into the
Promised Land.
Judges = Israel's leaders before
they had kings.
Ruth = she became David's great-
grandmother.

1&2 Samuel = the life of David
(from shepherd boy to king)
1&2 Kings = the history of Israel's
kings after David
(Civil War = North vs. South)
1&2 Chronicles = Records
(Chronicles) of the southern
kings (Judah)

Ezra = the temple in Jerusalem was
rebuilt after captivity
Nehemiah = the walls of Jerusalem
were rebuilt after captivity
Esther = how an orphaned Jewish
girl became Queen of Persia

III.

IV.

Instructions for Your Outline

> Write **Poetry** in the bottom left section of your outline, next to Roman numeral three (III). Next to Poetry put an **equal sign** followed by **5 Books**.

Job

> Underneath Poetry write the name of the first book, **Job**, followed by an **equal sign** and **A good man's faith perseveres thru very bad times**.

The book of Job addresses the issue of suffering.

Job gets its name from the main character in this book. He is **a good man** of integrity who seeks to please God with the way he lives his life. However, unbeknownst to Job, Satan is given permission to bring trials into Job's life to test his reverence of God. The first two chapters describe the extent of Job's suffering and make it clear that his suffering was not brought on by bad behavior. Also, Job is visited by three friends who seek to comfort him. They believe that God has caused trouble in Job's life because of his sin, for which he should repent. Over the course of several chapters the discussion between Job and his friends goes back and forth as his friends try to encourage Job to admit his sin and Job defends his integrity. Through this discussion each speaker gives his philosophy of life, suffering, and God's ways. At the end of the book, God speaks to Job, and restores Job with His full blessing. The reader of this book learns that God is sovereign even in times of suffering. Another lesson to learn is that all suffering is not a consequence of bad behavior: sometimes bad things happen to good people.

Psalms

> In the next line write **Psalms**, followed by an **equal sign** and **Prayers & songs of praise (mostly by David)**.

The book of Psalms reflects worship by one who is confident in the sovereignty of God.

Psalms are expressions of worship in the form of **prayers and songs of praise**. You will find a variety of emotions expressed with honesty and reverence for God. Some psalms give instruction; some were meant to be sung; and some psalms are prayers that could have been written in a prayer journal. One benefit of reading Psalms is that you will learn how to speak to God in prayer. Another benefit is that you will be reminded of God's goodness and blessings. You will also learn how to testify of these to others. If you were to peruse the 150 psalms, you would most likely find a psalm that matches your present emotions. Most of the psalms were written by David, many of which were written during difficult times in his life when he was forced to depend completely on God. This book has been a favorite for believers in every generation.

Proverbs

> In the next line write **<u>Proverbs</u>**, followed by an **<u>equal sign</u>** and **<u>Wise sayings on how to live wisely (by Solomon)</u>**.

Solomon became king of Israel after his father David's reign ended. Wanting to rule wisely for God, he asked God for wisdom. God gave him wisdom so that he became the wisest man who ever lived. People came from miles to hear his wisdom. A **proverb** is a brief saying that expresses **wisdom about life**. Solomon put these wise sayings in writing to help anyone who reads become wiser in the way they live. You will discover as you read these proverbs that wisdom and morality (obeying God's commands) go hand in hand. Proverbs is an excellent book for young people to read and thereby gain wisdom.

Ecclesiastes

> In the next line write **<u>Ecclesiastes</u>**, followed by an **<u>equal sign</u>** and **<u>A man's search for satisfaction (by Solomon)</u>**.

As king of Israel, **Solomon** had the wealth, power, and wisdom to **search for satisfaction** in the things of this world. Anyone who wishes for more wealth, more achievements, more fame, or more fun can follow Solomon's journey for satisfaction, which he recorded in **Ecclesiastes**. He discovered that all things that are found under the sun are vanity of vanities (or emptiness of emptiness). Instead of finding satisfaction or fulfillment, these things left him empty. His conclusion at the end of the book is to admonish his readers "to fear God and keep His commandments" (Eccl. 12:13). Ecclesiastes contains the memorable passage that begins, "To everything there is a season, a time for every purpose under heaven: a time to be born, a time to die…" (Eccl. 3:1-2).

The book of Ecclesistes wrestles with the subjects of satisfaction and fulfillment.

Song of Songs

The last book in the Poetry section was also written by Solomon.

> Write **<u>Song of Songs</u>**, followed by an **<u>equal sign</u>** and **<u>A song about marriage love (by Solomon)</u>**."

The **Song of Songs** captures the romantic excitement of the intimate love between a husband and wife. The Bible says that **Solomon** spoke 3,000 proverbs and 1,005 songs (1 Kgs. 4:32). This Song of Songs is devoted to **marriage**. An understanding of Israel's ancient culture and practices is necessary to appreciate the figures of speech in this book. Still, even a novice can grasp the romantic tone in each verse. Some Bibles refer to this book as **Song of Solomon**.

Instructions for Review

The exercises below serve to reinforce the information above and to help your memory. It will benefit you to say the names of the books out loud as you do each of the exercises. There are lists of the five books we have covered with open spaces for you to fill in the name of the missing book. It is important for you to remember the names of the books and the proper order. The second exercise requires you to put these books in their proper order, while saying their names out loud (i.e. #1 Job, #2 Psalms…). The third exercise requires that you match each theme with its book of the Bible by writing the correct letter in the blank. Every exercise should be spoken out loud as you complete them.

Old Testament Review
The Poetry Books: Job – Song of Songs

1. Fill in what is missing:

#1	#2	#3	#4	#5
Job	_____	Job	_____	_____
Psalms	_____	_____	Psalms	_____
Proverbs	_____	_____	Proverbs	_____
Ecclesiastes	Ecclesiastes	_____	_____	_____
Song of Songs	Song of Songs	_____	_____	_____

2. Put in the proper order: (Assign numbers 1-5)

#1	#2	#3
____ Job	____ Psalms	____ Ecclesiastes
____ Proverbs	____ Song of Songs	____ Proverbs
____ Psalms	____ Ecclesiastes	____ Songs of Songs
____ Song of Songs	____ Proverbs	____ Job
____ Ecclesiastes	____ Job	____ Psalms

3. Match the theme with the book of the Bible:

A. Job ____ Prayers and songs of praise (mostly by David).

B. Psalms ____ A song about marriage love (written by Solomon).

C. Proverbs ____ A good man's faith persevered through really bad times.

D. Ecclesiastes ____ A man's search for satisfaction (written by Solomon).

E. Song of Songs ____ Wise sayings on how to live wisely (written by Solomon).

Reading Assignment

When you have completed the exercises you will sample the Scriptures which we have studied. Your reading assignment is nine chapters: chapters 1-3 of Job, chapters 1, 22, and 23 of Psalms, chapter 10 of Proverbs, chapter 3 of Ecclesiastes, and chapter 1 of Song of Songs.

Job 1-3
Psalms 1, 22, 23
Proverbs 10
Ecclesiastes 3
Song of Songs 1

Here's a sneak preview of your reading assignment.

Job 1–3: This reading assignment will give you a sample from each of the books of Poetry. In Job you will read the narrative of how his trials came about and his response to them. You will encounter Hebrew poetry in the third chapter, which is the beginning of his first speech.

Psalms 1, 22, 23: In Psalms you will read three well known psalms. Psalm 1 testifies to the blessings of obeying God's law. Psalm 22 begins with a verse which was quoted by Jesus when He was crucified. It gives a description of what Jesus must have experienced on the cross, even though it was written 1000 years before He was born. Psalm 23 may be the most popular psalm.

Proverbs 10, Ecclesiastes 3, Song of Songs 1: Proverbs 10 gives a sample of the wise sayings collected in this book. Ecclesiastes 3 includes the passage made popular by the rock band of the 1960's, the Byrds. And Song of Songs 1 is a sample of the romantic love demonstrated in this book.

After you have completed your assignments, we will pick up with the next section of the Old Testament: the Prophets.

CHAPTER 4

The Prophets

In this chapter we will discuss the last seventeen books of the Old Testament, the books of the Prophets. Don't let the number seventeen intimidate you; our focus will be on just five! By way of review, each section so far has had its own particular genre (style of writing): commandments/instruction (law), historical narrative (history books), and poetry (poetry books). The prophetic books also have their own unique style of expression. The style of writing found in the prophetic books combines the urgency of personal persuasion with poetic expression. A prophet was a spokesman for God. God raised up prophets for the purpose of calling His people to repent of their sin and to return to God with their hearts. Prophetic messages carried warnings and exhortations to the Israelites of their day, but these messages also inform present day readers of God's future plans for mankind.

It is sometimes difficult to understand the prophet's message without knowing the contemporary issues that the prophet was addressing. However, even those who are reading the prophets for the first time will benefit from reading their message. Although some parts may be hard to understand, there is still great comfort and encouragement that can be taken from their writings. The prophets were passionate in their devotion to God and in their love for His holiness, which you will notice as you read.

A prophet was a spokesman for God. God raised up prophets for the purpose of calling His people to repent of their sin and to return to God with their hearts.

Old Testament Books

I. Law = 5 Books

Genesis = Beginnings
Creation, Fall, Flood, Promised Land,
Sodom & Gomorrah

Exodus = Way Out
10 Plagues, Red Sea,
10 Commandments, Tabernacle

Leviticus = Levi
Priests, sacrifices, Levites

Numbers = Counted
People numbered (2 million)
40 yrs in wilderness

Deuteronomy = 2nd Time
Moses' farewell sermons

II. History = 12 Books

Joshua = he led Israel into the
Promised Land.
Judges = Israel's leaders before
they had kings.
Ruth = she became David's great-
grandmother.

1&2 Samuel = the life of David
(from shepherd boy to king)
1&2 Kings = the history of Israel's
kings after David
(Civil War = North vs. South)
1&2 Chronicles = Records
(Chronicles) of the southern
kings (Judah)

Ezra = the temple in Jerusalem was
rebuilt after captivity
Nehemiah = the walls of Jerusalem
were rebuilt after captivity
Esther = how an orphaned Jewish
girl became Queen of Persia

III. Poetry = 5 Books

Job = A good man's faith
perseveres thru very bad times.

Psalms = Prayers & songs of praise
(mostly by David)

Proverbs = Wise sayings on how to
live wisely (by Solomon)

Ecclesiastes = A man's search for
satisfaction (by Solomon)

Song of Songs = A song about
marriage love (by Solomon)

IV. Prophets = 17 Books

A. _Major Prophets_ = 5 Books
  Isaiah (66)
  Jeremiah (52)
    Lamentations (5)
  Ezekiel (48)
  Daniel (12)

B. _Minor Prophets_ = 12 Books
  Hosea   Joel
  Amos   Obadiah
  Jonah   Micah
  Nahum   Habakkuk
  Zephaniah   Haggai
  Zechariah   Malachi

Old Testament Books

I. Law = 5 Books

Genesis = Beginnings
Creation, Fall, Flood, Promised Land,
Sodom & Gomorrah

Exodus = Way Out
10 Plagues, Red Sea,
10 Commandments, Tabernacle

Leviticus = Levi
Priests, sacrifices, Levites

Numbers = Counted
People numbered (2 million)
40 yrs in wilderness

Deuteronomy = 2nd Time
Moses' farewell sermons

II. History = 12 Books

*Joshua = he led Israel into the
Promised Land.*
*Judges = Israel's leaders before
they had kings.*
*Ruth = she became David's great-
grandmother.*

*1&2 Samuel = the life of David
(from shepherd boy to king)*
*1&2 Kings = the history of Israel's
kings after David
(Civil War = North vs. South)*
*1&2 Chronicles = Records
(Chronicles) of the southern
kings (Judah)*

*Ezra = the temple in Jerusalem was
rebuilt after captivity*
*Nehemiah = the walls of Jerusalem
were rebuilt after captivity*
*Esther = how an orphaned Jewish
girl became Queen of Persia*

III. Poetry = 5 Books

*Job = A good man's faith
perseveres thru very bad times.*

*Psalms = Prayers & songs of praise
(mostly by David)*

*Proverbs = Wise sayings on how to
live wisely (by Solomon)*

*Ecclesiastes = A man's search for
satisfaction (by Solomon)*

*Song of Songs = A song about
marriage love (by Solomon)*

IV.

Instructions for Your Outline

We will group the books of this section into two parts: the **Major Prophets** and the **Minor Prophets**. This designation is not related to importance; rather it is related to the number of chapters. The Major Prophets have more content; the Minor Prophets have fewer chapters. You will be encouraged to memorize the order of the five books of the Major Prophets, but we will settle for just a familiarity with the twelve Minor Prophets.

> Write **The Prophets** in the bottom right section of your paper, next to Roman numeral four (IV). Next to "The Prophets" put an **equal sign** (=), followed by **17 Books**. Underneath write **A. Major Prophets** and underline it. About halfway down toward the bottom of this section write **B. Minor Prophets** and underline it.

Prophetic messages carried warnings and exhortations to the Israelites of their day, but these messages also inform present day readers of God's future plans for mankind.

Major Prophets

> Under "Major Prophets" write **Isaiah (66)**. The prophetic book of Isaiah is a compilation of messages which the prophet Isaiah received from God. There are **66 chapters** in this book.

Isaiah shares an interesting similarity with the whole Bible. The Bible has 66 books, which are divided into two parts: 39 Old Testament books and 27 New Testament books. Isaiah has 66 chapters, which also seem to be divided into two parts: 39 chapters which emphasize judgment for sin, followed by 27 chapters which emphasize salvation. Isaiah lived 700 years before Jesus Christ was born. Yet, he was able to foretell specific features of Jesus' birth, ministry, and sacrificial death (Isa. 7:14; 9:6-7; 53:1-12; 61:1-3). Your Bible Reading assignment will include Isaiah 53, which describes the suffering of the Messiah.

> Under "Isaiah" write **Jeremiah (52)**.

The prophet **Jeremiah** lived about 600 years before Christ was born. During this time Israel declined spiritually. Jeremiah's message called the Israelites to repentance and warned them of the consequences of ignoring God. The Israelites continued to ignore God and even mistreated His prophet Jeremiah. The end result of their spiritual decline was the invasion of their nation by Babylon and the destruction of Jerusalem and the temple. Jerusalem was destroyed by the Babylonians in 586 BC. Jeremiah foretold that the captivity would last 70 years (Jer. 25:11). God also revealed to him the hope of the New Covenant (Jer. 31:31-34). There are **52 chapters** in this book.

Under "Jeremiah" write **Lamentations (5)**.

This short book is included with the Major Prophets because Jeremiah was the author. To **lament** is to cry and wail. Jeremiah's description of the destruction of Jerusalem because of the sin of its people called for lamentation. There are only **five chapters** in this book.

On the next line write the next Major Prophet, **Ezekiel (48)**.

The prophet **Ezekiel** was one of the Jews who was taken into captivity and exiled to Babylon. His messages include rebukes for the sins of idolatry, injustice, and wickedness, but also messages of hope for the return of God's glory among His people. Ezekiel has **48 chapters**.

The last Major Prophet to write on your outline is: **Daniel (12)**.

Daniel was a young man who was exiled to Babylon and his book spans many years. He lived under the reigns of both Babylonian and Persian kings. The Persians conquered the Babylonians. He was a capable man who served in the administrations of both of these foreign governments. But above all he was a man of God and a prophet. The first six chapters of this book present an historical record of major events of his life, including the account of the fiery furnace and the lion's den. The second half of the book has an apocalyptic style which uses symbolism to foretell future events in God's plan for human history. Your Bible reading assignment will include Daniel 6, which is the account of Daniel in the lion's den.

The prophets were passionate in their devotion to God and in their love for His holiness.

Minor Prophets

Underneath "Minor Prophets" you make two lists of six names each for the twelve Minor Prophets. In the first list write **Hosea, Joel, Amos, Obadiah, Jonah, and Micah**. In the second list write **Nahum, Habakkuk, Zephaniah, Haggai, Zechariah, and Malachi**. Also, put **a circle around Jonah** in the first column and **a circle around Daniel** in the Major Prophets. This is because these two prophetic books are written in narrative form making them very enjoyable to read. Your reading assignment includes reading the four chapters of Jonah.

Instructions for Review

The following exercises will help you to remember the information you have just learned about the Major and Minor Prophets. It will benefit you to say the names of the books out loud as you complete each of the exercises.

In the first exercise are four lists of the seventeen books of the prophets, both the Major and Minor Prophets. Fill in the name of the missing books in the open spaces, one list at a time. Start at the top of each list and say the name of the book out loud as you go down the list, filling in the open spaces as you go. The second exercise requires that you circle the names of only the Major Prophets in each of the four lists. Every exercise should be spoken as you do them.

Old Testament Review

The Prophets (17 Books)

1. Fill in what is missing:

#1	#2	#3	#4
Isaiah	Isaiah	_____	_____
Jeremiah	_____	Jeremiah	_____
Lamentations	Lamentations	_____	_____
Ezekiel	_____	Ezekiel	_____
Daniel	Daniel	_____	_____

Hosea	_____	Hosea	_____
Joel	_____	Joel	_____
Amos	_____	Amos	_____
Obadiah	_____	Obadiah	_____
Jonah	_____	Jonah	_____
Micah	_____	Micah	_____
Nahum	Nahum	_____	_____
Habakkuk	Habakkuk	_____	_____
Zephaniah	Zephaniah	_____	_____
Haggai	Haggai	_____	_____
Zechariah	Zechariah	_____	_____
Malachi	Malachi	_____	_____

2. Circle the 5 "Major Prophets" (Isaiah, Jeremiah, Lamentations, Ezekiel, Daniel):

#1	#2	#3	#4
Hosea	Hosea	Hosea	Hosea
Joel	Daniel	Isaiah	Joel
Isaiah	Joel	Jeremiah	Amos
Amos	Amos	Joel	Obadiah
Obadiah	Obadiah	Amos	Isaiah
Jeremiah	Ezekiel	Obadiah	Jeremiah
Jonah	Jonah	Jonah	Lamentations
Micah	Micah	Micah	Jonah
Lamentations	Lamentations	Lamentations	Micah
Nahum	Nahum	Nahum	Nahum
Habakkuk	Jeremiah	Habakkuk	Ezekiel
Ezekiel	Habakkuk	Zephaiah	Habakkuk
Zephaniah	Zephaniah	Ezekial	Zephaniah
Haggai	Haggai	Daniel	Daniel
Zechariah	Zechariah	Haggai	Haggai
Daniel	Malachi	Zechariah	Zechariah
Malachi	Isaiah	Malachi	Malachi

Reading Assignment

Now it is time to sample the Scriptures of the Prophets. Your reading assignment is nine chapters: chapters 9 and 53 of Isaiah, chapters 3, 5 and 6 of Daniel, and chapters 1-4 of Jonah.

Isaiah 9, 53
Daniel 3, 5, 6
Jonah 1-4

Isaiah 9, 53: The assigned passages in Isaiah will give you a flavor of the prophetic style of expression. As you read, listen for the poetry and the passion in his message. In Isaiah 9 you will read a popular Christmas Scripture that is tied to the birth of the Son of David (the Messiah), who's rule will never end. The description of this king shows he is more than human. Christians see a clear fulfillment of prophecy in the birth of Jesus Christ. When you read Isaiah 53, take note of the description of the Messiah's suffering and death for the sins of the people. After the birth and death of Jesus Christ, these two passages became more clear and meaningful. It is indeed a wonder how Isaiah foresaw these things 700 years before Jesus was born! The prophets were able to foretell the future because God revealed it to them. God is all-knowing. He knows the future as well as the past and present.

Daniel 3, 5, 6 & Jonah 1-4: The assigned reading in Daniel and Jonah will allow you to see that these two books were written in a narrative style, which is not the typical form for the prophetic books. God's message to his people is revealed in the life experiences of his servants which are recorded in these two books. In the three chapters in Daniel you will read about three events that have left a lasting legacy in the English language. You will read the stories of the "fiery furnace," the "handwriting on the wall," and the "lion's den." In Jonah you will read about a man swallowed by a great fish and he lived to tell about it.

It will benefit you to finish reading these chapters before continuing on with the next outline. Completing each reading assignment will help you remember the location of each book and will give you an idea of the content of this section of the Bible.

After you have completed your assignments, we will begin a new outline: Old Testament People. The next outline will follow the story line of significant people in the Old Testament from the beginning to the end. This will help you to see how the Old Testament books and the events recorded in them all fit together.

Part 2
Old Testament People

Old Testament People

Our first outline introduced you to the books of the Old Testament and showed how these books are grouped together in our Bibles. You should now be able to locate any Old Testament book in the Bible by remembering in which of the four sections it is found: Law, History, Poetry, or Prophets.

This second outline follows the storyline of the Old Testament. Its focus is on the significant people you will encounter as you read through the Old Testament books. As we follow the storyline you will see how the books of the Old Testament fit together as a whole. You will also discover that the God of the Bible is a personal God who chose to reveal Himself through His relationships and interactions with His covenant people.

In this section you will write another **outline** focusing on significant **people of the Old Testament**! Your finished outline will look like the outline on the next page. Your outline will divide Old Testament history into four time periods: Creation to the Flood, the Patriarchs, the Nation of Israel, and the Kingdom of Israel.

The next four chapters will provide information about significant people in each of the four historical time periods of the Old Testament, before the coming of Jesus Christ. Your outline will identify the four time periods and will show the connection of these time periods with the corresponding books of the Old Testament. And because these people are historical personalities, you will be given approximate dates to locate their lives on the timeline of human history. Let's get started.

Old Testament People

I. Creation to Flood

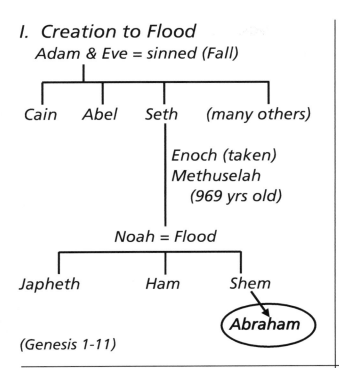

Adam & Eve = sinned (Fall)

Cain   Abel   Seth   (many others)

Enoch (taken)
Methuselah
(969 yrs old)

Noah = Flood

Japheth   Ham   Shem

(Abraham)

(Genesis 1-11)

II. <u>Patriarchs</u> = Forefathers of a chosen people

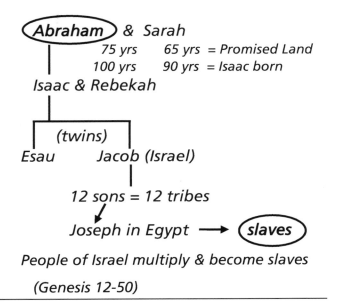

(Abraham) & Sarah

75 yrs   65 yrs = Promised Land
100 yrs   90 yrs = Isaac born

Isaac & Rebekah

(twins)
Esau   Jacob (Israel)

12 sons = 12 tribes

Joseph in Egypt ⟶ (slaves)

People of Israel multiply & become slaves

(Genesis 12-50)

III. <u>Nation</u> of Israel

Moses = Deliverance from (slavery)

- raised by Pharaoh's daughter
- 40 yrs Prince, 40 yrs Shepherd, 40 yrs Prophet
- had a brother named Aaron (Aaron & descendants = priests)

Joshua = Conquest of Promised Land
- leader after Moses
- land divided among 12 tribes

Judges = raised up to deliver the people from oppression resulting from sin

Ruth = remarried widow from Moab
- becomes the great-grandmother of (King) David

(Exodus - Ruth)
(1525 BC - 1050 BC = 475 yrs)

IV. <u>Kingdom</u> of Israel

Saul = 1ˢᵗ (King) of Israel

David = 2ⁿᵈ King (killed Goliath)
     man after God's heart

Solomon = 3ʳᵈ King (David's son)
- wisest man
- temple built

Civil War = North vs. South
     (Israel vs. Judah)

(Many kings)   (Prophets)

Captivity = taken out of land (70 yrs)
Return to Promised Land

Ezra   Daniel
Nehemiah   Esther   (Prophets)

(1 Samuel - Malachi)
(1050 BC - 400 BC = 650 yrs)

CHAPTER 5

Creation to Flood

In this chapter we will introduce some significant people who lived during the first time period of human history. As the title states this time period begins with **Creation** and ends with the **Flood**. These people's life stories are told in the first eleven chapters of Genesis. Because the people in this section are linked by a genealogy, you will be making a family tree that reflects their relationships and the sequence of time.

Instructions for Your Outline

> Next to Roman numeral one in the top left section of your outline, write **Creation to Flood**. Underneath "Creation" write **Adam + Eve = sinned (Fall)**. Use the figure on the next page to guide you.

The first people created by God were **Adam and Eve**. God made them in His image and likeness. What are some ways that human beings are like God? This is not a reference to physical traits because God is spirit. Human beings are different from animals in that humans have an eternal soul. There is a part of us that continues to exist after we die. It is that part of us that is the real us, made in God's image. Like God, humans are able to discern morality (righteousness and truth); to communicate and understand abstract ideas; to appreciate and create beauty; to reason, plan, and dream; and to love voluntarily. God made us like Himself so that we can know Him and enjoy a relationship with Him that lasts forever!

But the consequences of Adam and Eve's sin hurt their relationship with each other and with God. **Sin** is the disobedience of God's commands. God told Adam that the consequence of sin was death: "You will surely die" (Gen 2:17). Death entered the world through the sin of Adam and Eve. Additionally, and tragically, Adam and Eve were affected spiritually by their sin: sin became part of their nature. This sin nature, which shows itself in selfishness, is passed from one generation to the next. And ever since, everyone who has been born is born a sinner.

God made us like Himself so that we can know Him and enjoy a relationship with Him that lasts forever!

Old Testament People

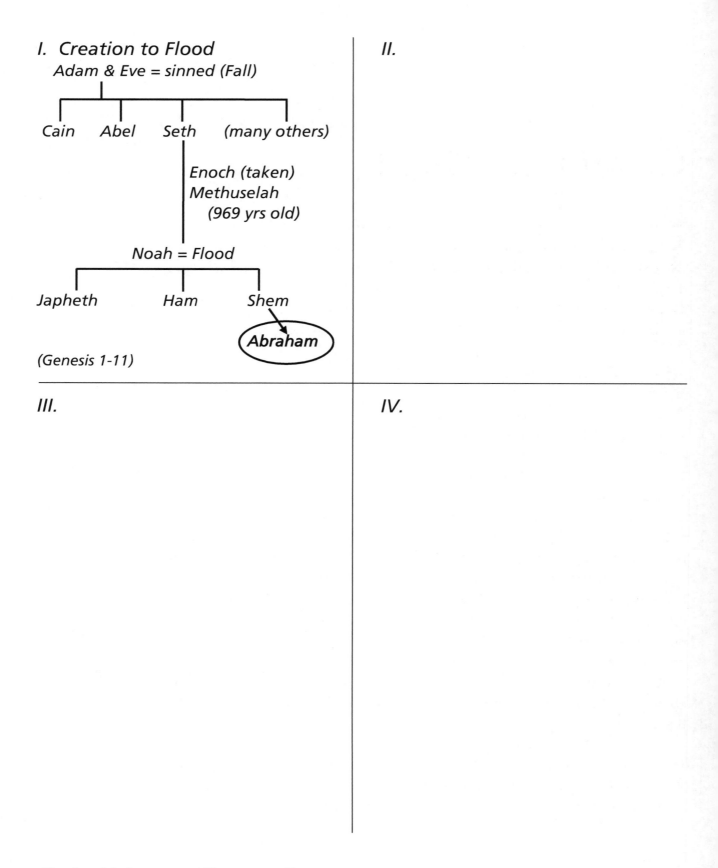

I. **Creation to Flood**

Adam & Eve = sinned (Fall)

Cain   Abel   Seth   (many others)

Enoch (taken)
Methuselah
(969 yrs old)

Noah = Flood

Japheth   Ham   Shem

Abraham

(Genesis 1-11)

II.

III.

IV.

Old Testament People

I.

II.

III.

IV.

> Draw a "family tree" down from Adam + Eve that branches out to the following names: **Cain**, **Abel**, **Seth**, and **many others**. (See the figure on the previous page for guidance.) Draw a line under "Seth" downward about two inches and write **Noah** underneath, followed by an **equal sign (=)** and **flood**.

Although it is popular today to say that people belong to various races, the Bible makes it clear that there is only one race: the human race. If you go back far enough, we are all related. The ethnic differences of appearance, language and culture are minor and do not cancel out our common ancestry and the fact that every single person is created in God's image.

Adam and Eve's first children were **Cain and Abel**. Out of envy Cain killed his brother Abel. Cain's act of murder is evidence of having inherited the sin-nature from his parents. Adam and Eve had **many other children**, but **Seth** is significant because Noah was his descendant. The Bible records the genealogy from Adam to Noah in Genesis 5. During Noah's lifetime God caused a worldwide **flood** that destroyed all living things on the earth. The flood was God's judgment for man's sinfulness. Only Noah and his family, along with two of every kind of animal, survived the flood because they were kept safe on the ark.

> In the space between "Seth" and "Noah" draw a branch half way down and write **Enoch (taken)**. Underneath "Enoch" draw another branch and write **Methuselah (969 yrs old)**.

In the genealogy of Genesis 5 the names of Adam's descendants down to Noah are listed, along with the number years they lived. Lifespans before the flood were very long. **Methuselah** (Enoch's son) was the oldest man who ever lived: **he lived 969 years!** Maybe you've heard the expression that someone is "as old as Methuselah?" **Enoch** is significant because he did not die. After living 365 years, during which he walked with God, Enoch was **taken** by God. God brought Enoch right into His presence, without experiencing death.

> Draw a tree down from Noah that branches out for three names: **Japheth**, **Ham**, and **Shem**. Under "Shem" draw an arrow downward, and beneath the arrow write the name of **Abraham**. Draw a circle around "Abraham" because he will be our link to the next section.

Noah had three sons: **Japheth**, **Ham**, and **Shem**. All three sons and their wives survived the flood by living on the ark with Noah and his wife. For an entire year the flood waters covered the whole earth. Everyone living today is a descendant of Noah and his three sons. Although it is popular today to say that people belong to various races, the Bible makes it clear that there is only one race: the human race. If you go back far enough, we are all related. The ethnic differences of appearance, language and culture are minor and do not cancel out our common ancestry and the fact that every single person is created in God's image.

The differences of language and culture can be traced back to when the descendants of Noah's sons dispersed at the time of the Tower of Babel. The Indo-European language family would be associated with the descendants of Japheth. The Semitic languages (which include Hebrew and Arabic) are associated with the descendants of Shem (as the similarity of the name indicates). Abraham was a descendant of Shem, which is why Jews (descendants of Abraham) are called Semites.

Everyone living today is a descendant of Noah and his three sons.

> On the line at the bottom of this section write **(Genesis 1-11)**. You will find the people mentioned in this section in the first eleven chapters of Genesis.

Instructions for Review

The three exercises on the next page are designed to help you remember the names of the people we covered in this section. In the first exercise you will match each person's name with the description by writing the correct letter in the blank by each name. In the second exercise you will write out three lists of the names of the people from the first exercise. And in the third exercise you will write out the description for each of the names listed. Use the descriptions you were given in the first exercise. Complete the review exercises before proceeding to the reading assignment that follows.

Old Testament Review

Significant People: Creation – Flood

1. Match the person with the description:

    ___ Adam   A. A descendant of Shem but who Jewish people refer to as father

    ___ Eve   B. A son of Noah and father of Semitic peoples

    ___ Cain   C. He was told to build an ark because of a coming Flood

    ___ Noah   D. He killed his brother Abel

    ___ Shem   E. The first one created, from whom we inherited our sin nature

    ___ Abraham   F. Adam's wife, "the mother of all the living"

2. Write the above names in three columns:

      #1   *#2*   *#3*

3. Write the description for each of the names listed:

    Adam:

    Eve:

    Cain:

    Noah:

    Shem:

    Abraham:

Reading Assignment

Now it is time to sample the Scriptures which we have studied. Your reading assignment is nine more chapters in Genesis. You will read chapters 12, 21-22, 28-30, 37, 39-41.

Genesis 12, 21-22, 28-30, 37, 39-41

Genesis 12, 21-22, 28-30, 37, 39-41: As you will recall, Genesis is the first book of the "Law," also referred to as the "Torah." We refer to the writing style, or genre, of Genesis as historical narrative. Narrative makes for interesting reading and is a very effective form of teaching. Though narrative is associated with story, it is important to remember that the events recorded in the Bible actually happened in human history. Reading the assigned chapters will introduce you to the "Patriarchs" of the nation of Israel, the chosen people of God. You will discover how God chose Abraham, a man of faith, and made an everlasting covenant with him and his descendants (Gen 12). You will learn about the miraculous birth of his son, Isaac, who was used to test Abraham's faith (Gen 21-22). You will see how God affirmed his covenant with Isaac's son, Jacob, who fathered twelve sons (Gen 28-30). And you will gain insight about trials from the experience of one of Jacob's sons, Joseph (Gen 37,39-41). These chapters in Genesis will prepare you for the next section of your outline.

After you have completed your assignments, we will pick up with the next section of the Old Testament People: the Patriarchs.

CHAPTER 6

The Patriarchs

This chapter will familiarize you with the **Patriarchs of God's chosen people**, the nation of Israel. Patriarchs are **forefathers** who provide an identity for their descendants who come after them. When God appeared to Moses on Mount Sinai, He referred to Himself as the God of Abraham, Isaac, and Jacob; these are the patriarchs of the Israelites. The historical record of how God chose the Israelites to be his own special people is found in Genesis. It begins with the Patriarchs, with whom God made and affirmed His everlasting covenant.

After the flood, the families who descended from Noah's three sons were scattered by God because He gave them different languages at the tower of Babel (Genesis 11). You will recall that **Abraham** descended from Shem, the son of Noah. Abraham is our link to this chapter because he is the first patriarch and the founding father of the Israelites. From the twelfth chapter of Genesis on, the rest of the book of Genesis records significant events in the lives of the patriarchs.

Patriarchs are forefathers who provide an identity for their descendants who come after them.

Instructions for Your Outline

Next to Roman numeral two (II) in the top right section of your outline, write **Patriarchs**, followed by an **equal sign (=)** and **Forefathers of a chosen people**. Underneath "Patriarchs" write **Abraham + Sarah**. Use the figure on the next page to guide you. Circle "Abraham" to show the link with the previous section of your outline.

Underneath "Abraham" draw a line downward about an inch long; under the line write **Isaac + Rebekah**. Directly under "Abraham" (and to the right of the line) write **75 yrs**. And directly under "Sarah" write **65 yrs**, followed by an **equal sign (=)** and **Promised Land**. Directly underneath "75 yrs" write **100 yrs** and under "65 yrs" write **90 yrs**, followed by an equal sign and **Isaac born**.

Old Testament People

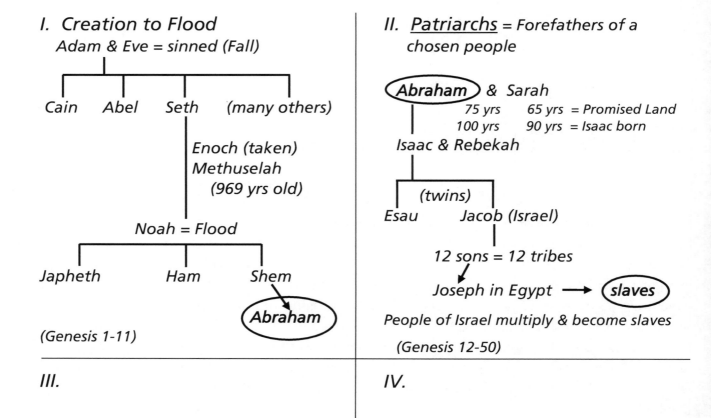

I. Creation to Flood

Adam & Eve = sinned (Fall)

Cain   Abel   Seth   (many others)

Enoch (taken)
Methuselah
(969 yrs old)

Noah = Flood

Japheth   Ham   Shem

Abraham

(Genesis 1-11)

II. Patriarchs = Forefathers of a chosen people

Abraham & Sarah

75 yrs   65 yrs = Promised Land
100 yrs   90 yrs = Isaac born

Isaac & Rebekah

(twins)

Esau   Jacob (Israel)

12 sons = 12 tribes

Joseph in Egypt ⟶ slaves

People of Israel multiply & become slaves

(Genesis 12-50)

III.

IV.

Old Testament People

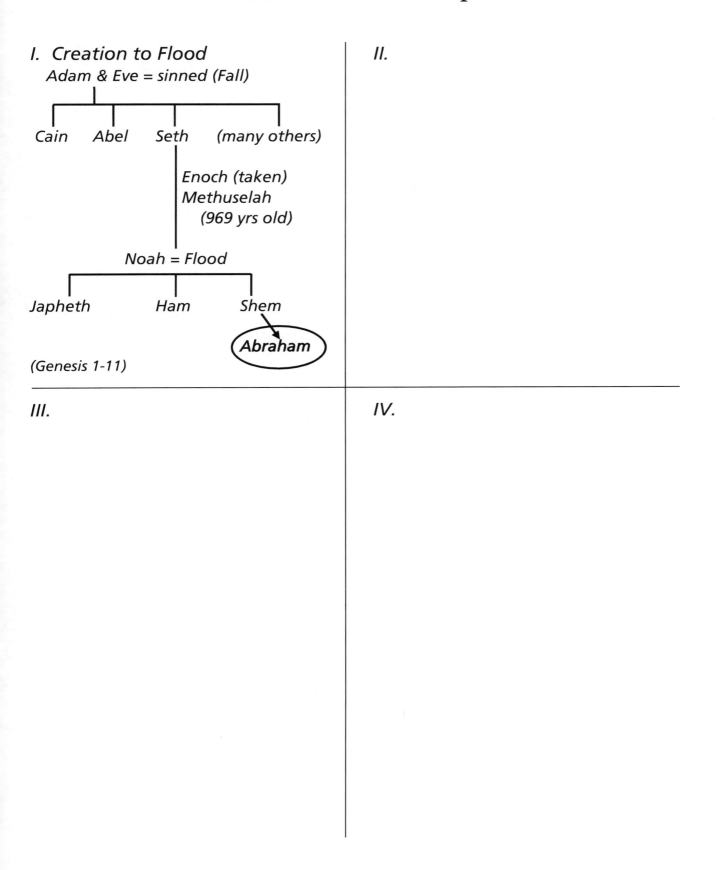

I. **Creation to Flood**
    Adam & Eve = sinned (Fall)

    Cain   Abel   Seth   (many others)

                    Enoch (taken)
                    Methuselah
                        (969 yrs old)

                Noah = Flood

    Japheth   Ham   Shem

                                (Abraham)

    (Genesis 1-11)

II.

III.

IV.

In your last reading assignment you read how God called Abram to leave his family and country and go to a land where God would make of him a great nation (Genesis 12). (God would eventually change his name from Abram to Abraham, and Sarai's name to Sarah.) The promises God made to Abraham were unconditional and were affirmed in a covenant with Abraham and his descendants. God promised to Abraham land (the Promised Land), many descendants, and that all the nations of the world would be blessed through him. **Abraham and Sarah** demonstrated faith in God's word by traveling many miles to the land of Canaan, a place they had never seen before and which was already inhabited by other nations. Abraham was **75 years old** and Sarah was **65 years old** when they came to the **Promised Land**.

Patriarchs are forefathers who provide an identity for their descendants who come after them.

In order to be the father of a great nation Abraham needed children, but his wife Sarah was not able to have children, and was past the time for childbearing. In an attempt to help God with His promise, Sarah came up with the idea that her husband should impregnate her slave girl, Hagar. This led to the birth of Ishmael, who is the father of the Arab people. Even today, many Arab nations are hostile toward the people of Israel. But God waited until it was humanly impossible for Sarah to become pregnant. **Abraham was 100 years old** and **Sarah was 90 years old when Isaac was born!** Abraham's faith is revealed in the Bible by his obedience to God; and because of his faith God called him His friend.

Isaac is called the son of promise (Galatians 4:23) because he is the son God promised to Abraham. God confirmed with Isaac the covenant he made with Abraham. After the death of his mother, Sarah, Isaac married his wife. Her name was **Rebekah**.

> On your outline, continue the family tree by drawing a line downward under "Isaac" about an inch. At the bottom of the line, draw a family tree that branches out for two names; under the left branch write <u>Esau</u>; under the right branch write <u>Jacob (Israel)</u>. Between the two branches write <u>(twins)</u>.

Isaac's wife Rebekah gave birth to **twin** sons: the firstborn was **Esau**, followed by **Jacob**. When they were in the womb God had revealed to Rebekah that the older would serve the younger. It was custom for the oldest son to be given the greater share of the inheritance. However, when the boys were older, Esau sold his birthright to Jacob for a pot of stew at a time when he was very hungry. And near the time of their father Isaac's death, when he was blind from old age, Jacob impersonated his brother and obtained his father's blessing which he intended to give Esau. Because of this, Esau hated his brother, Jacob, and wanted to kill him. God however reaffirmed His covenant with Jacob. This was the same covenant he made with Abraham and Isaac. And God changed Jacob's name to **Israel**. After wrestling with God Jacob became a new man, just as his new name indicated. Jacob's descendants would forever be known as the people of Israel. In modern history, the people of Israel

God changed Jacob's name to Israel.

were recognized as a nation again in 1948, in the land God promised to Abraham, Isaac, and Jacob (Israel).

On your outline, under "Jacob" draw a line downward about an half inch; under the line write **12 sons = 12 tribes**. Underneath "12 sons" draw a line diagonally toward the corner about an inch; under this line write **Joseph in Egypt => slaves**. Circle the word "slaves". Underneath "slaves" write **multiply & become slaves**. And at the bottom of this section (just above the boundary line) write **(Genesis 12-50)**.

Jacob, fearing Esau's intent to kill him, left the Promised Land. He returned to the land of his mother to search for a wife among her relatives. He met Rachel and fell in love with her. However her father, like Jacob, was a con-man. Although Jacob worked seven years for Rachel, her father substituted the older sister as the bride under the covering of the wedding veil.

Jacob woke up to this surprise the day after the wedding. He had worked seven years for Rachel, but ended up with her sister Leah. Rachel's father agreed to give her to Jacob in a week's time, but only if he worked another seven years for her. This caused much strife in the family as Leah was not loved by Jacob and she had to compete with her sister Rachel for his attention. And Leah could bear children, but Rachel could not. So Rachel offered her slave-girl as a way to provide offspring for her husband. Then Leah made the same offer to Jacob with her slave-girl. Then Rachel became pregnant with her first child. Jacob, with four wives, ended up in a short time with twelve sons and one daughter. These **twelve sons** of Jacob (Israel) became the fathers of the **twelve tribes** of Israel.

Sorrow was no stranger to Jacob's family. Rachel was the favored wife, which his other wives resented. Rachel's firstborn son was **Joseph**. Rachel was excited about her pregnancy because it meant that she could bear Jacob more children. And sure enough, another pregnancy followed. However, she experienced hard labor and died shortly after giving birth to her second son, Benjamin. Because Rachel was Jacob's first love and his favorite wife, he treated her son Joseph better than all of his brothers. One example of special favor was Jacob's gift of a multicolored coat to Joseph. This favoritism caused Joseph's brothers to despise him and become bitter.

While shepherding their father's vast herds, the brothers conspired to kill Joseph when he was far from their father's watchful care. But instead of killing him a better plan conveniently developed when a caravan of merchants passed their way. They sold Joseph for pieces of silver to the merchants who were headed to Egypt. They then tore the fancy coat and dipped it in the blood of a goat to make it seem as if Joseph was torn to pieces by a wild animal. That was the story they told their father. They were not prepared for how deeply their father grieved, even refusing to be comforted.

The twelve sons of Jacob (Israel) became the fathers of the twelve tribes of Israel.

But Joseph replied, "Don't be afraid of me. Am I God, that I can punish you? You intended to harm me, but God intended it all for good. He brought me to this position so I could save the lives of many people." (Gen. 50:19-20 NLT)

Meanwhile Joseph was sold as a **slave** to one of Pharaoh's officials. The Pharaoh was the king of Egypt. Joseph found himself in a foreign land where the people spoke an unfamiliar language. He lost his father, his family, and his freedom. But God was with Joseph through all of his trials. When Joseph was promoted by his master because of his wisdom and industry, his master's wife cast her eye on him. When Joseph refused to be seduced, she falsely accused him to her husband who angrily put him in prison. In prison, Joseph interpreted the dreams of two of Pharaoh's servants. When Pharaoh was deeply bothered by dreams that made no sense to his wisemen, Pharaoh's servant remembered how Joseph had accurately interpreted their dreams. Joseph was called out of prison and, after interpreting Pharaoh's dreams, was made Prime Minister of Egypt.

Genesis records the irony of Joseph's meeting with his brothers, the very ones who betrayed him. They traveled a long distance from the Promised Land to buy grain during a severe famine. Twenty years had passed since they last saw him as a teenager. They did not recognize him, and he kept his identity secret from them. When he did reveal himself to them, he invited his brothers to bring their families to Egypt where he could provide for them throughout the severe famine that would last seven years.

Jacob, his sons, and his sons' families traveled to Egypt and settled in the best land. Jacob was overcome with joy when he learned that his son Joseph was still alive. He found strength in his old age as he looked forward to his reunion with Joseph.

God took a bad situation in Joseph's life and used it for good in the lives of many. And Joseph, who could have been bitter and vengeful toward his brothers, forgave them and protected them. The people of Israel **multiplied** in Egypt. However, after Joseph's death another Pharaoh who didn't know Joseph saw the Israelite people as a threat to the security of Egypt. **He enslaved** the Israelites and forced them into hard labor. They cried out to God and waited for God to deliver them. God heard their groans and sent them a deliverer named Moses.

Instructions for Review

There are three exercises on the following page which are designed to help you remember the names of the people who were covered in this section. In the first exercise you will match the person with the description by placing the correct letter in the blank by each name. In the second exercise you will write the names of the people who are listed in the first exercise into three lists. And in the third exercise you will write out the description for each of the names listed, which are provided in the first exercise.

Old Testament People

Significant People: The Patriarchs

1. Match the person with the description:

____ Abraham   A. Jacob's twin brother, who gave up his birthright for a pot of stew

____ Sarah   B. Abraham's long-awaited son

____ Isaac   C. His brothers sold him out, but God turned it for good

____ Esau   D. He had 12 sons and his name was changed to Israel

____ Jacob   E. Abraham's wife, who gave birth when she was 90 yrs old

____ Joseph   F. The king of Egypt

____ Pharaoh   G. A man known for his faith, God promised him a land and a son, and called him His friend

2. Write the above names in three columns:

     #1   #2   #3

3. Write a description for each of the names listed:

Abraham:

Sarah:

Isaac:

Esau:

Jacob:

Joseph:

Pharaoh:

Reading Assignment

Your reading assignment is in Exodus, the book which follows Genesis.

Exodus 1-4, 7-8, 11-14

Exodus 1-4, 7-8, 11-14: By way of review, Exodus is the second book of the "Law." The first section of the Bible consists of five books, which are known as the "Law" or "Torah" or "the Pentateuch." All five of these books were written by Moses, a man who was instrumental in Israel becoming a nation. In your reading assignment you will learn about Moses' humble birth, his privileged upbringing as a prince of Egypt, and his exile as a shepherd (Exodus 1-4). On the backside of a desert, Moses heard God speak in a burning bush. God sent him to Egypt to lead the people of Israel out of slavery. Pharaoh, the king of Egypt, needed some persuading to release the Israelites, which came in the form of ten plagues (Exodus 7-8). The final plague was connected to the institution of the Passover Sacrifice, which became a yearly memorial of God's deliverance of His people (Exodus 11-14). The Israelites left Egypt in a hurry. By the power of God they passed through the Red Sea on dry ground! These chapters in Exodus (way out) will prepare you for the next section of your outline.

When you have completed your assignments, we will begin the next section pertaining to Old Testament People: the Nation of Israel.

CHAPTER 7

Nation of Israel

In this chapter you will become familiar with significant people who lived during the time period when the tribes of Israel became the **nation of Israel**. Nations distinguish themselves by the laws which unify them as a people, and by leaders whose authority is recognized nationally. National leaders, common laws, and a geographical location, along with a unifying religion and language, all give a nation its unique identity. Under Moses' leadership Israel became a nation. They worshiped the one true God and obeyed His commands, which were written in the Hebrew language. Under the leadership of Moses and Joshua the nation of Israel settled into the land which God promised to the patriarchs Abraham, Isaac, and Jacob. This promise became the hope of Jacob's twelve sons and their descendants.

The present-day nation of Israel would not exist today were it not for the miraculous intervention of God in human history.

This time period begins after the death of Jacob and his sons, while their descendants, the Israelites, are enslaved in Egypt. In that foreign land they multiplied but remained a collection of tribes until God raised up Moses to lead them out of Egypt. The powerful plagues that God brought upon the Egyptians through Moses made him a national hero and leader. On the way to the Promised Land, at Mount Sinai, God gave His people laws which contributed to their identity as a nation under God. The commands governed ceremonial matters of worship, civil matters of citizenship, and matters of morality. The Israelite government was a theocracy with God as their true leader. The present-day nation of Israel would not exist today were it not for the miraculous intervention of God in human history! We will follow this time period from Israel's deliverance from slavery in Egypt under Moses, to settling into the Promised Land under Joshua, and to the temporary leadership of Judges. This time period ended when God consented to install Israel's first king.

Old Testament People

I. Creation to Flood

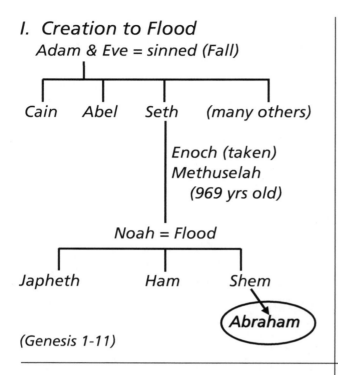

Adam & Eve = sinned (Fall)

Cain   Abel   Seth   (many others)

Enoch (taken)
Methuselah
(969 yrs old)

Noah = Flood

Japheth   Ham   Shem

Abraham

(Genesis 1-11)

II. Patriarchs = Forefathers of a chosen people

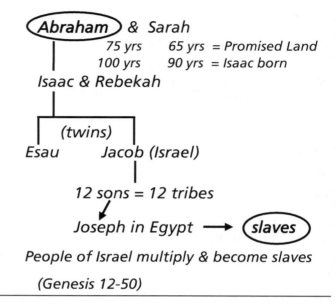

Abraham & Sarah

75 yrs	65 yrs	= Promised Land
100 yrs	90 yrs	= Isaac born

Isaac & Rebekah

(twins)
Esau   Jacob (Israel)

12 sons = 12 tribes

Joseph in Egypt ⟶ slaves

People of Israel multiply & become slaves

(Genesis 12-50)

III. Nation of Israel

Moses = Deliverance from slavery
- raised by Pharaoh's daughter
- 40 yrs Prince, 40 yrs Shepherd, 40 yrs Prophet
- had a brother named Aaron (Aaron & descendants = priests)

Joshua = Conquest of Promised Land
- leader after Moses
- land divided among 12 tribes

Judges = raised up to deliver the people from oppression resulting from sin

Ruth = remarried widow from Moab
- becomes the great-grandmother of King David

(Exodus - Ruth)
(1525 BC - 1050 BC = 475 yrs)

IV.

Old Testament People

I. Creation to Flood

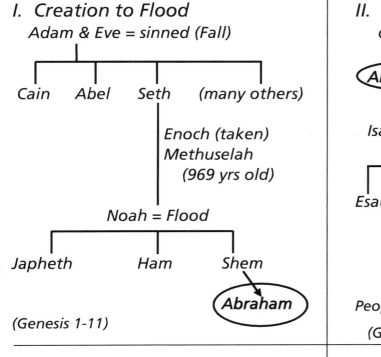

Adam & Eve = sinned (Fall)

Cain   Abel   Seth   (many others)

Enoch (taken)
Methuselah
(969 yrs old)

Noah = Flood

Japheth   Ham   Shem

Abraham

(Genesis 1-11)

II. <u>Patriarchs</u> = Forefathers of a chosen people

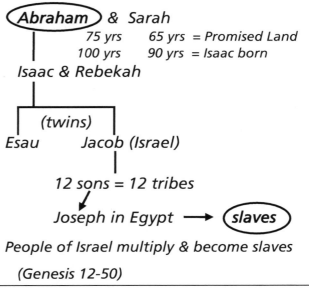

Abraham & Sarah

| 75 yrs | 65 yrs | = Promised Land |
| 100 yrs | 90 yrs | = Isaac born |

Isaac & Rebekah

(twins)
Esau   Jacob (Israel)

12 sons = 12 tribes

Joseph in Egypt → slaves

People of Israel multiply & become slaves

(Genesis 12-50)

III.

IV.

Instructions for Your Outline

Nation of Israel

> Next to Roman numeral three ("III") in the bottom left section of your outline, write **Nation of Israel** and underline the word "Nation." The nation of Israel came into existence through the supernatural power of God. God intervened in human history so that He could accomplish His plan of redemption, which would involve working through a special nation: the nation of Israel.

Moses

> Underneath "Nation" write **Moses** followed by an **equal sign (=)** and **Deliverance from slavery**. Circle the word "Slavery" to show the connection with the ending of the previous section (the Patriarchs). Under "Moses" write **raised by Pharaoh's daughter**. Under this write **40 yrs Prince, 40 yrs Shepherd, 40 yrs Prophet** (try to write small enough to include all of this on the same line if possible). On the next line under this write **had a brother named Aaron**. Then on the next line write in parentheses **(Aaron & descendants = priests)**.

There is no understating how important Moses' role is in Israel's history.

There is no understating how important **Moses'** role is in Israel's history. In your last reading assignment you read about Moses' birth in Egypt. When Moses' mother could no longer hide him safely (because of the king's command that Hebrew baby boys be put to death), she set her three month old baby in a water-proofed basket on the river, where he was discovered by **Pharaoh's daughter**, who adopted him as her own. Growing up in the Egyptian palace, Moses received the best education. But he never forgot his Israelite roots. This got him in trouble later on when he killed an Egyptian taskmaster who was abusing some Israelite slaves. When it was discovered what Moses had done he fled far from the sovereignty of Egypt to the land of Midian. He was **40 years old**.

In the land of Midian Moses became a shepherd and married a sheik's daughter. At the **age of 80**, while he was shepherding his father-in-law's flock, Moses heard God speak to him from a burning bush. God sent him back to Egypt to d**eliver the Israelites, God's people, from slavery**. Moses' **older brother, Aaron**, supported and encouraged Moses when he confronted Pharaoh, the king of Egypt. After Egypt was devastated by the Ten Plagues, Pharaoh let the Israelites leave Egypt. When Pharaoh changed his mind and sent his army after them, God opened the Red Sea for the Israelites to pass through on dry ground. And when the army of chariots chased after them through the sea, God brought the waters of the sea crashing down on them and destroyed the Egyptian army.

God chose **Aaron, Moses' brother**, to be the Israelites' first **priest**. Only priests were permitted to offer sacrifices to God. And only **Aaron and his sons, and their descendants**, could be priests throughout Israel's history. Moses and Aaron belonged to the tribe of Levi. The rest of the tribe of Levi (**the Levites**) served as assistants to the priests, both in temple service and in teaching God's law to the people. The book **Leviticus** means pertaining to the Levites; it explains the ceremonial requirements of worship which were under the supervision of the priests and Levites. (See Appendix: Abraham – Aaron Family Tree.)

God met with Moses face to face on Mount Sinai. After receiving God's commands and instructions on Mount Sinai, Moses led the Israelites to the Promised Land. And even though the Israelites had watched as God's power delivered them from Egypt, and in spite of the miraculous provision of food and guidance by God's presence, the Israelites constantly complained against Moses and God. And when the Israelites finally rebelled and intended to return to Egypt, God put to death the leaders of the rebellion and punished the people by extending their journey in the wilderness **40 years**. When the older generation who rebelled died in the wilderness, Moses brought the Israelites to the edge of the Promised Land. Just before he died, Moses reminded them of all that God did for them and all that God said to them. He reminded them of these things in his final farewell sermons, which are recorded in the book of Deuteronomy. Moses died at the age of **120 years**; he had lived **40 years as a Prince of Egypt, 40 years as a Shepherd, and 40 years as a prophet or spokesman for God**!

Moses died at the age of 120 years; he had lived 40 years as a Prince of Egypt, 40 years as a Shepherd, and 40 years as a prophet or spokesman for God!

Joshua

On your outline, begin a new line and write **Joshua** followed by an **equal sign (=)** and **Conquest of Promised Land**. Underneath "Joshua" write **leader after Moses**. Underneath this write, **land divided among 12 tribes**.

Joshua was chosen by God to lead the Israelites into the Promised Land after Moses died. The land God promised to Israel was occupied by Canaanite nations who had lived there many years and who had fortified cities. But under Joshua's leadership and with the help from Almighty God, the tribes of Israel were victorious in the **Conquest of the Promised Land**. After conquering the major power centers, Joshua **divided the land among the 12 tribes of Israel**. This is how the land of Canaan became the land of Israel. These events are recorded in the book of Joshua, which is located in the history section of the Old Testament. You have already read the first three chapters of Joshua in your reading assignments.

Judges

> On your outline, on a new line write **Judges** followed by an **equal sign (=)** and **raised up to deliver the people from oppression resulting from sin**.

This cycle of sin => oppression => repentance => deliverance (by a Judge) occurs several times over a period of about 350 years.

After Joshua died the people of Israel lacked national leadership. It wasn't long before many Israelites began to forsake God's commands and adopt the immoral customs of the Canaanites, who had been judged by God for their wickedness. God's people were doing whatever was "right in their own eyes," but their actions were not right in God's eyes. As punishment for breaking His covenant, God removed His protection of Israel, which allowed neighboring nations to oppress the Israelites. **Oppression** caused the Israelites to **recognize their sin** and to call out to God for **deliverance**. God answered their prayers by **raising up leaders who led the Israelites to victory and freedom from oppression**. These leaders were called **Judges**.

This cycle of sin => oppression => repentance => deliverance (by a Judge) occurs several times over a period of about 400 years. An earlier Scripture reading assignment acquainted you with **Gideon and Samson** in the book of Judges. With only 300 men, **Gideon defeated an army of over 100,000**! He and his men shouted, "The sword of the Lord and of Gideon!" **Samson** was given supernatural strength to fight against the enemies of Israel. One part of Samson's vow required that he not cut his hair. His downfall happened as a result of revealing this secret to a woman he thought he loved, who then cut his hair while he was sleeping, making him weak. The last judge was Samuel, who is mentioned in the book named after him. (Hints are underlined for your review exercises.)

Ruth

> Getting back to your outline, begin a new line and write **Ruth** followed by an **equal sign (=)** and **a remarried widow from Moab**. Under this write, **becomes the great-grandmother of King David**. Then Circle the word "King" because this will be our connection with the next section: the Kingdom of Israel.

By now you should be familiar with **Ruth,** having read all four chapters in the book about her life. Ruth was not an Israelite; she was from the neighboring country of Moab. The Moabites descended from Abraham's nephew Lot. However, Ruth married into an Israelite family from Bethlehem. After becoming a widow, she chose to go back to Bethlehem with her widowed mother-in-law. Her faith and character were displayed when she said, "Your people will be my people, and your God, my

God" (Ruth 1:16). While caring for her mother-in-law, Ruth remarried a prominent man from the tribe of Judah, named Boaz, and gave birth to a son. Through this son **Ruth became the great-grandmother of King David**, Israel's greatest king and the ancestor of the Messiah!

Ruth lived during the time of the Judges. Her life story shows that not all Israelites turned their backs on God. And her life is a testimony to the faithfulness of God to everyone who trusts in Him, especially the weak and insignificant.

Date

> Under "Ruth," write **(Exodus – Ruth)**. Next to that write **(1525 BC – 1050 BC = 475 yrs)**. Hopefully you have enough room at the bottom of this section to include this information.

The Exodus occurred around 1445 BC, which is 1,445 years before the birth of Christ (BC = before Christ).

The time period of "the Nation of Israel" began with the birth of Moses (**1525 BC**), which was 80 years before the Exodus. The Exodus occurred around 1445 BC, which is 1,445 years before the birth of Christ (BC = before Christ). After the Exodus, the Israelites wandered for 40 years in the wilderness before arriving at the Promised Land. After Moses died, Joshua led the Israelites in the conquest of the Promised Land that God promised to Abraham. After Joshua died, Israel found deliverance and leadership under the Judges. The next period in Israel's history began with the installation of Israel's first king, which happened around **1050 BC**. You will find the events of this time period recorded in the four books of the law: **Exodus, Leviticus, Numbers, and Deuteronomy**; and continuing in the history books: **Joshua, Judges, and Ruth**. These events spanned about 475 years.

Instructions for Review

The three exercises which follow are designed to help you remember the names of the people we covered in this section. In the first exercise you will match the person with their description by placing the correct letter in the blank by each name. In the second exercise you will write the names of the people in the first exercise in three lists. And in the third exercise you will write out the description for each of the names listed. These are the descriptions that are given in the first exercise.

Old Testament People

Significant People: The Nation of Israel

1. Match the person with the description:

    ___ Moses   A. The strongest man in the world until his hair was cut

    ___ Aaron   B. Moses' brother, he and his sons became the first priests

    ___ Joshua   C. With only 300 men he defeated an army of over 100,000

    ___ the Judges   D. He led the Israelites out of Egypt after ten devastating plagues

    ___ Gideon   E. He led the Israelites into the Promised Land after Moses died

    ___ Samson   F. A remarried widow from Moab, King David's great-grandmother

    ___ Ruth   G. Israel's leaders before they had kings

2. Write the above names in three columns:

    #1   #2   #3

3. Write a description for each of the names listed:

    Moses:

    Aaron:

    Joshua:

    The Judges:

    Gideon:

    Samson:

    Ruth:

Reading Assignment

Your reading assignment is to read 1 Kings 17-18; 2 Chronicles 36; Esther 1-4; Malachi 3-4.

I Kings 17-18
2 Chronicles 36
Esther 1-4
Malachi 3-4

The Scriptures in this assignment will give you a glimpse of the events which will happen in the next time period in Israel's history: the Kingdom of Israel. In the next chapter you will learn about the division of the kingdom into a northern and southern kingdom. In this assignment you will read about the ministry of **Elijah** the prophet **(1 Kings 17-18)**, who ministered during the time of the evil King Ahab of the northern kingdom.

In **2 Chronicles 36** you will read about the conquering of the southern kingdom by the Babylonians and the destruction of Jerusalem, its capital city. The Babylonians took the people of Judah into Captivity in Babylon. The captivity was a forced exile of those who survived the destruction of Jerusalem to Babylon. The remains of the ancient city of Babylon are today found in Iraq.

The events in the book of Esther take place during the time of captivity in the land of Persia, which today we know as Iran. **Esther**, an orphaned Jewish girl, became the Queen of Persia. You will read her amazing story in **Esther 1-4**, and you will learn the significance of her Jewish identity.

The Persians allowed the Jews who were exiled to return to the land of Israel. The prophet **Malachi** was the last of the Old Testament prophets in Israel's history. He ministered about 400 years before Jesus Christ was born. When you read **Malachi 3-4** you will gain a sense of the expectation that the Jewish people had of the coming of the Messiah.

When you complete your assignments, we will begin the next section in our study Old Testament People: the Kingdom of Israel.

CHAPTER 8

Kingdom of Israel

As we follow the story line through Israel's history we come to the fourth and last time period of the Old Testament and the final section of your outline: the **Kingdom of Israel**. In this chapter you will become familiar with significant Old Testament people who lived during this time period when kings ruled Israel.

God originally established the nation of Israel as a theocracy with God as Israel's ruler and king. But even though they shared a common faith, heritage, religion, language, and laws, the Israelites did not experience national unity. Rather, they continued to function as self-interested tribes. They believed that this self-interest was the cause of their vulnerability to foreign invaders. But in reality, it was their disobedience to God's commands that led to their troubles, as the book of Judges reveals. So a desire grew among the people to establish a monarchy in Israel, a king who could unite the nation to defend itself.

The desire for a king was not a bad thing in itself. In fact, in his farewell speech (Deuteronomy), Moses revealed that a king was part of God's future plan (Deut. 17:14-20). However, the Israelites' motives for wanting a king were wrong. Their desire came from their lack of faith in God's rule and in their desire to be like all the other nations, who did not know the living and true God. And even though their motive for wanting a king was wrong God consented to Israel's request because, in light of God's future plans, it was His will that Israel have a king.

With the installment of a king, Israel became a kingdom. The first kings were chosen by God. To signify God's choice, the king was anointed with oil by a priest or prophet. The designated king became known as "the anointed one," which in the Hebrew tongue is "messiah," but in Greek is "christ." In time God would reveal His plan that through the kingdom of Israel He would establish the kingdom of God on earth under the rule of His Anointed One: the Messiah (or Christ) of God, the King of kings and Lord of lords! The prophets foretold that this coming Messiah would be a descendant of King David and His kingdom would be one of righteousness and peace! In the New Testament we will learn that Jesus is the Christ, the Son of David!

The first kings were chosen by God. To signify God's choice, the king was anointed with oil by a priest or prophet. The designated king became known as "the anointed one," which in the Hebrew tongue is "messiah," but in Greek is "christ."

Old Testament People

I. Creation to Flood

Adam & Eve = sinned (Fall)

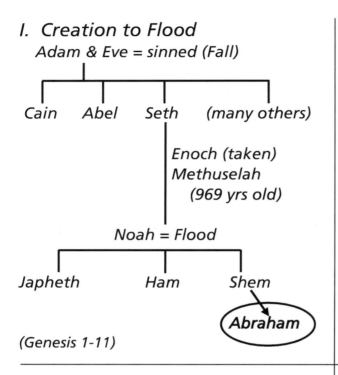

Cain   Abel   Seth   (many others)

Enoch (taken)
Methuselah
(969 yrs old)

Noah = Flood

Japheth   Ham   Shem

(Abraham)

(Genesis 1-11)

II. <u>Patriarchs</u> = Forefathers of a chosen people

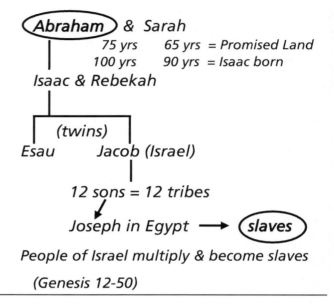

(Abraham) & Sarah
 75 yrs   65 yrs = Promised Land
100 yrs   90 yrs = Isaac born
Isaac & Rebekah

(twins)
Esau   Jacob (Israel)

12 sons = 12 tribes

Joseph in Egypt ⟶ (slaves)

People of Israel multiply & become slaves

(Genesis 12-50)

III. <u>Nation</u> of Israel

Moses = Deliverance from (slavery)
- raised by Pharaoh's daughter
- 40 yrs Prince, 40 yrs Shepherd, 40 yrs Prophet
- had a brother named Aaron (Aaron & descendants = priests)

Joshua = Conquest of Promised Land
- leader after Moses
- land divided among 12 tribes

Judges = raised up to deliver the people from oppression resulting from sin

Ruth = remarried widow from Moab
- becomes the great-grandmother of (King) David

(Exodus - Ruth)
(1525 BC - 1050 BC = 475 yrs)

IV. <u>Kingdom</u> of Israel

Saul = 1st (King) of Israel

David = 2nd King (killed Goliath)
         man after God's heart
Solomon = 3rd King (David's son)
- wisest man
- temple built
Civil War = North vs. South
            (Israel vs. Judah)

(Many kings)   (Prophets)

Captivity = taken out of land (70 yrs)
Return to Promised Land
Ezra   Daniel
Nehemiah   Esther   (Prophets)

(1 Samuel - Malachi)
(1050 BC - 400 BC = 650 yrs)

Old Testament People

I. Creation to Flood

Adam & Eve = sinned (Fall)

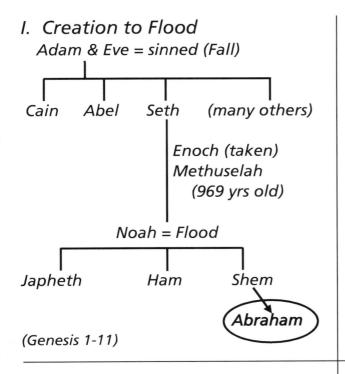

Cain   Abel   Seth   (many others)

Enoch (taken)
Methuselah
    (969 yrs old)

Noah = Flood

Japheth   Ham   Shem

Abraham

(Genesis 1-11)

II. *Patriarchs* = Forefathers of a chosen people

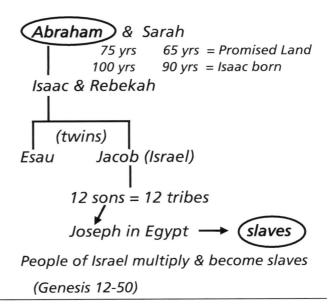

Abraham & Sarah

| 75 yrs | 65 yrs | = Promised Land |
| 100 yrs | 90 yrs | = Isaac born |

Isaac & Rebekah

(twins)

Esau   Jacob (Israel)

12 sons = 12 tribes

Joseph in Egypt ⟶ slaves

People of Israel multiply & become slaves

(Genesis 12-50)

III. Nation of Israel

Moses = Deliverance from slavery
- raised by Pharaoh's daughter
- 40 yrs Prince, 40 yrs Shepherd, 40 yrs Prophet
- had a brother named Aaron (Aaron & descendants = priests)

Joshua = Conquest of Promised Land
- leader after Moses
- land divided among 12 tribes

Judges = raised up to deliver the people from oppression resulting from sin

Ruth = remarried widow from Moab
- becomes the great-grandmother of King David

(Exodus - Ruth)
(1525 BC - 1050 BC = 475 yrs)

IV.

The events and people of this time period are recorded in the Old Testament books from 1 Samuel (in the history section) to Malachi (the last book in the prophet section). The dates are from about 1050 BC to about 400 BC, which is around 650 years.

Instructions for Your Outline

Kingdom of Israel

Next to Roman numeral four ("IV") in the bottom right section of your outline, write **Kingdom of Israel** and underline the word "Kingdom."

Israel's well-being was determined by their king's commitment to obeying God's will. Israel thrived under righteous kings who honored, worshiped, and trusted God. And when Israel's kings despised God and did not follow His laws, the kingdom struggled and suffered many problems.

Israel became a kingdom with the anointing of Saul which established Israel as a monarchy. Leadership is very important to the welfare of any organization. Israel's well-being was determined by their kings' commitment to obeying God's will. Israel thrived under righteous kings who honored, worshiped, and trusted God. And when Israel's kings despised God and did not follow His laws, the kingdom struggled and suffered many problems. The history of Israel's kings is found in 1 & 2 Kings.

Saul

Underneath "Kingdom" write **Saul** followed by an **equal sign (=)** and **1st King of Israel**. Circle the word "King" to show the connection with the reference to King David at the bottom of the previous section, the Nation of Israel.

God chose **Saul** to be the **first king of Israel**. Saul was from the tribe of Benjamin. He appeared to be everything that the people were looking for: he stood head and shoulders above others. Unfortunately, Saul had difficulty obeying God's commands, which was a reflection of the condition of his heart, and was more important than his appearance. Though Saul ruled for forty years, his reign was filled with trouble with the neighboring nation of the Philistines. He died in battle against the Philistines.

David

On your outline, begin a new line and write **David** followed by an **equal sign (=)** and **2nd King (killed Goliath)**. Underneath "2nd King" write **man after God's heart**.

When God rejected Saul as king, He sent Samuel to anoint **David** to be the next king (**2ⁿᵈ king**), because David was a **man after God's heart**. Even as a young man, David wanted to please God with all of his life. David was from the tribe of Judah. David demonstrated his faith when he fearlessly volunteered to fight the Philistine champion, Goliath. In your earlier assignment you read how David faced Goliath, a real giant, on the battlefield. Goliath stood ten feet tall and David's only weapon was his sling. But God gave David the victory because of his faith; and he **killed Goliath**.

David ruled as king for 40 years. During his reign Israel expanded its borders and subdued its enemies. Because of David's love for God, God made an eternal promise to David that his son, one of his own descendants, would rule from his throne forever! This is a reference to the Messiah, who in the New Testament is called the "Son of David." David was not a perfect man; his adultery with Bathsheba is recorded in 2 Samuel 11-12. But he was sincere in his faith, as demonstrated by his repentance. Evidence of God's forgiveness is found in God's choice of Solomon to succeed David as king. Solomon's mother was Bathsheba, the woman with whom he committed adultery and afterward married. (Review: You will find the record of David's life in 1 & 2 Samuel.)

Because of David's love for God, God made an eternal promise to David that his son, one of his own descendants, would rule from his throne forever! This is a reference to the Messiah, who in the New Testament is called the "Son of David."

Solomon

> On your outline, begin another new line and write **Solomon** followed by an **equal sign (=)** and **3rd King (David's son)**. Draw a line down from "David" to "Solomon" to show that Solomon is David's son. Under "3rd King" write **wisest man**; and under this write **temple built**.

God revealed to David that his son, **Solomon**, would rule as **king after him**. And this began David's dynasty which continued until the Babylonian Captivity. All of the kings who reigned in Jerusalem after David were his descendants and, therefore, belonged to the tribe of Judah. (Review: The history of all of the kings of Judah is recorded in 1 & 2 Chronicles.)

At the beginning of his reign, Solomon was very careful to honor the Lord, just as his father David had. So God appeared to Solomon in a dream and gave him permission to make any request. Whatever Solomon asked for God would grant it. Solomon requested understanding and discernment from God in order to rule God's people wisely. Solomon's request pleased God. He had not asked for long life, or riches, or the death of his enemies. God not only gave Solomon what he asked for, but also gave him the things for which he did not ask. **Solomon became wiser than any man** and his fame was known widely. People came from far away lands just to hear him. First Kings 3:32 reveals that he wrote 3,000 proverbs and 1,005 songs. And Solomon wrote the poetry books of Proverbs, Ecclesiastes, and Song of Songs.

With his wisdom and wealth, Solomon kept the promise he made to his father David to **build a temple** for God in Jerusalem. The Ark of the Covenant which was housed in a tent prior to this was moved to the temple. The temple, as the place where one came to worship and honor God through ritual sacrifice, played a central role in the religious lives of the Israelites.

Civil War

On your outline, begin a new line and write **Civil War** followed by an **equal sign (=)** and **North vs. South**. Under this write, **(Israel vs. Judah)**. Draw a straight line down from "Solomon" to "Civil War."

The northern tribes chose their own king and were called the Kingdom of Israel. The descendants of David reigned as kings of the southern kingdom, which was called the Kingdom of Judah.

Later in his life, Solomon turned away from following God whole-heartedly because of the idolatry of his many foreign wives. God confronted Solomon with prophets and foretold His punishment. During the reign of Solomon's son, God would divide the kingdom of Israel into two kingdoms, leaving Solomon's descendants to rule over two tribes. This came about early in the reign of Solomon's son. A disagreement led to a **Civil War** which divided the ten tribes of the **North** from the two tribes of the **South**. The northern tribes chose their own king and were called the **Kingdom of Israel**. The descendants of David reigned as kings of the southern kingdom, which was called the **Kingdom of Judah**. Judah remained the predominant tribe because of its size and its connection to David. (Review: the events of the kings of both Israel and Judah are recorded in 1 & 2 Kings which is in the history section.)

Captivity

On your outline; draw a wiggly line down from "Civil War" about an inch. Under this line write **Captivity** followed by an **equal sign (=)** and **taken out of land (70 yrs)**. Above "Captivity" write, **(many kings)** on the left side of the wiggly line. Across from this on the other side of the wiggly line write, **(Prophets)**.

The prophets called the people to repent of their sin and to return to God. They foretold both God's coming judgment and the comforting news of the coming Messiah.

After the Civil War divided the tribes into two kingdoms, **many kings** in succession ruled in both the northern and southern kingdoms. The highlights of their reigns are found in 1 & 2 Kings. Also during this time God raised up **Prophets** to speak to the people in both kingdoms. True prophets were men of God who spoke the messages God gave them. The prophets called the people to repent of their sin and to return to God. They foretold both God's coming judgment and the comforting news of the coming Messiah. Their messages are found in the books of the Prophets in the Old Testament.

After many warnings and calls to repentance, God's judgment came first to the northern Kingdom of Israel. At this time the capital city of the northern kingdom was called Samaria. The Assyrians conquered the northern kingdom. They removed the survivors from the land and scattered them throughout their empire. The Assyrians brought peoples from other nations to live in the land of Israel. These people intermarried with the Israelites who were allowed to remain in the northern kingdom. Their descendants are called "Samaritans" in the New Testament. The southern Kingdom of Judah remained faithful longer than their brethren in the north. But in time their idolatries and immoralities met with God's judgment at the hands of the Babylonians. God foretold that the **Babylonian Captivity** would last **70 years**. The army of Babylon destroyed Jerusalem, both its walls and its temple, and killed many of its inhabitants. Those who survived were taken captive to Babylon. There they settled and lived, keeping their customs and their faith alive. (Your assigned reading in 2 Chronicles 36 gives you a description of this sad time.)

Return to Promised Land

> Begin a new line on your outline and write, **Return to Promised Land**. You will need the little space you have left in this section to write three lines of more names. To the left of this section write **Ezra** and underneath that write **Nehemiah**. To the right of these two names write **Daniel** and underneath write **Esther**. And further right of that, write **(Prophets)**.

When the Persians defeated the Babylonians, the Persian king gave permission for the Jews to return to their home land. Many Jews (from Judah) **returned to the Promised Land**, but not all. They found Jerusalem in ruins. The rebuilding of the temple was their first priority upon their return to Jerusalem. Ezra the priest recorded this historic achievement. **Ezra** taught the people God's law after their return from exile. The Israelites next priority was to rebuild the walls of Jerusalem. But hostile neighbors stopped that work leaving Jerusalem defenseless. **Nehemiah**, a Jew who had a prominent position in the Persian administration, asked God to give him favor with the Persian king. God granted that request when the Persian king gave his support to the effort to finish rebuilding the city walls. The rebuilding of Jerusalem's walls is recorded in the book of Nehemiah (found in the section of the History Books).

Daniel was a teen when the Babylonians carried him away to Babylon. He lived through the captivity, and never returned to his home in Jerusalem. He served in both the Babylonian and Persian governments. Daniel was a prophet of God. His book is located in the Bible with the Major Prophets. **Esther** became queen of Persia during the reign of the Persian king Xerxes. Her life story takes place just before the time of Ezra and Nehemiah. (Your recent reading assignment included Esther 1-4.)

The last three Minor **Prophets** (Haggai, Zechariah, and Malachi) **ministered in the Promised Land after the Israelites' return from Captivity**. Malachi lived about **400 BC** and he was the last prophet to speak in the Old Testament. His message concluded with an expectation of the sudden coming of the Messiah. After him

"This entire land will become a desolate wasteland. Israel and her neighboring lands will serve the king of Babylon for seventy years. Then, after the seventy years of captivity are over, I will punish the king of Babylon and his people for their sins," says the LORD. "I will make the country of the Babylonians a wasteland forever." (Jer. 25:11-12 NLT)

So the message of the LORD spoken through Jeremiah was fulfilled. The land finally enjoyed its Sabbath rest, lying desolate until seventy years were fulfilled, just as the prophet had said. (2 Chron. 36:21 NLT)

came 400 years of silence until the day God sent His angels to announce the coming of the Savior, Jesus Christ (Messiah), the Lord (See Luke 2:11).

(1 Samuel – Malachi)
(1050 BC – 400 BC = 650 yrs)

> At the very bottom of this section write **(1 Samuel – Malachi) (1050 – 400 BC = 650 yrs)**.

The Exodus occurred around 1445 BC, which is 1,445 years before the birth of Christ (BC = before Christ).

This period of Israel's history touches most of the books of the Old Testament. In the <u>history section</u> of the Old Testament, the books from **1 Samuel to Esther** took place during this period of time. All of the <u>poetry books</u> except Job (**Psalms to Song of Songs**) were written by David and Solomon. Most of the Psalms were written by David. And all of <u>the prophets</u> whose messages are preserved in our Scriptures lived during the time of the Kingdom of Israel (**Isaiah to Malachi**). This period began with the anointing of Saul as king around **1050 BC** and concluded with the ministry of Malachi around **400 BC**, which is about **650 years**. Here are some other approximate dates for significant events mentioned in this section: David became king – 1000 BC; Temple built by Solomon – 960 BC; Destruction of Jerusalem & Captivity – 600 BC. (These dates are rounded.)

Congratulations, you have now completed both outlines for the Old Testament! The first outline helped familiarize you with the books of the Old Testament. To test your memory continue to review your outline until you can list the books of each section in their correct order. You should also be able to locate any Old Testament book in your Bible now that you know which section it belongs to and which books come before and after it. The second outline which we just completed has familiarized you with significant people of the Old Testament. We followed the story line through each time period of the Old Testament so that you can see how the Old Testament books fit together.

Instructions for Review

The three exercises which follow are designed to help you remember the names of the people we covered in this section. In the first exercise you will match the person with their description by placing the correct letter in the blank by each name. In the second exercise you will write the names of the people in the first exercise into three lists. And in the third exercise you will write out the description for each of the names listed. These descriptions are given in the first exercise.

Old Testament People

Significant People: The Kingdom of Israel

1. Match the person with the description:

    ____ Saul   A. Israel's second king, a man after God's heart

    ____ David   B. Israel's first king

    ____ Solomon   C. The name of the Southern Kingdom after the civil war split

    ____ Kingdom of Israel   D. The name of the Northern Kingdom after the civil war split

    ____ Kingdom of Judah   E. Israel's third king, known for his wisdom

    ____ the Prophets   F. He ended up in the lion's den

    ____ Daniel   G. Men of God who spoke the messages God revealed to them

    ____ Ezra   H. An orphaned Jewish girl who became Queen of Persia

    ____ Nehemiah   I. He led in the rebuilding of the walls of Jerusalem

    ____ Esther   J. He taught the people God's law after the return from exile

2. Write the above names in three columns:

    #1   #2   #3

3. Write a description for each of the names listed:

Saul:

David:

Solomon:

Kingdom of Israel:

Kingdom of Judah:

Daniel

Ezra:

Nehemiah:

Esther:

Reading Assignment

For your next reading assignment you will read Acts 7; Luke 1-2; Matthew 1-2, 5-7; John 1-3.

Acts 7

Luke 1-2

Matthew 1-2, 5-7

John 1-3

As you can see from your reading assignment we will now turn our attention to the New Testament! In **Acts 7** you will read the words of Stephen as he gives a defense for his faith just before he was martyred. This chapter is helpful to you because Stephen gives an overview of Israel's history from the time of the patriarchs to the time of Moses, as Israel became a nation, and on to the time of Israel's kings and the building of the temple.

The other readings are from three of the gospels. In **Luke 1-2** you will read the account of Jesus' birth from Mary's perspective, which includes the announcements of the angels and visit by the shepherds. In **Matthew 1-2** you will read about Jesus' birth from Joseph's perspective, which includes the coming of the wise men. Compare these accounts with the Christmas story you heard while growing up.

In **Matthew 5-7** you will read Jesus' Sermon on the Mount, which will give you a sampling of Jesus' teaching. And in **John 1-3** you will read of Jesus' first encounters with several people at the beginning of His ministry. Among these people are John the Baptist, Jesus' first disciples, and a religious leader named Nicodemus.

When you have completed your assignments, we will be ready to begin your last outline: the New Testament Books.

Part 3
New Testament Books

New Testament Books

When we began this study we stated that the Scriptures written before Christ's coming are contained in the Old Testament. The New Testament begins with the coming of Jesus Christ. He is the messenger and mediator of a new covenant between God and His people. Moses was the mediator of the old covenant; Jesus is the mediator of the new covenant. The old and new testaments take their names from their relationships to these covenants.

These next chapters are your instructions for making your outline for all of the **books of the New Testament**. When you have completed your outline it will look like the figure on the next page. Your outline will group the New Testament books into four sections: the Gospels, Acts, the Epistles, and Revelation. Each chapter gives you information for the books in that section and explains why they are grouped together.

As you become familiar with the NT books you will discover a variety of literary styles. The Gospels and Acts are written in a narrative style. The Epistles employ an epistolary style that you would expect for letters written to churches and to individuals. And the last book, Revelation, is a prophetic book written with an apocalyptic style. We are now ready to begin your study of the Gospels.

New Testament Books

(Good News)
I. Gospels = 4 Books

Matthew = tax collector, apostle
- wise men follow star (2)
- Sermon on the mount (5-7)

Mark = young man

Luke = physician
- shepherds at the stable (2)
- Parables: Good Samaritan (10), Rich Fool (12), Prodigal Son (15), Lazarus & Rich man (16)

John = fisherman, apostle
- 7 "I am" sayings (6:48; 8:12; 10:9,11; 11:25; 14:6; 15:5; 8:58)
- 7 miracles
- Key verses 3:3; 3:16; 14:6; 20:28; 20:31

Read what Jesus said & did
➡ Understand who He is & why He came ➡ Good News!!

II. Acts = 1 Book
(themes)

1. Gospel (Acts 1:8) Jerusalem ➡Judea ➡ Samaria ➡ ends of earth
   a) What is the gospel message?
   b) To whom is the gospel to be told?
   c) What response does the gospel call for?
2. The Church
   a) How are churches started?
   b) What do churches do?
   c) What is a good/healthy church?
3. The Holy Spirit
   a) Who is the Holy Spirit?
   b) How important is the Holy Spirit?
   c) How is the Holy Spirit received?

III. Epistles (Letters) = 21 Books

A. *Paul's Letters*
   1. Romans
   2. 1 Corinthians
   3. 2 Corinthians
   4. Galatians ⎤ Go
   5. Ephesians ⎟ Eat
   6. Philippians⎟ Pop-
   7. Colossians ⎦ corn
   8. I Thessalonians
   9. 2 Thessalonians
   10. 1 Timothy ⎤
   11. 2 Timothy ⎬ Pastoral
   12. Titus ⎦ Epistles
   13. Philemon

   (5 T's — 8–12)

B. *General Letters*
   1. Hebrews   5. 1 John
   2. James   6. 2 John
   3. 1 Peter   7. 3 John
   4. 2 Peter   8. Jude

IV. Revelation = 1 Book
(themes)

Future = how human history will end

Encouragement for believers = your faith will be rewarded! (on winning side!)

Reckoning & Judgment

Eternity = salvation complete
- damnation for God-haters (gospel-rejecters)

CHAPTER 9

The Gospels
Good News

The first four books of the New Testament are known as the Gospels. The titles of the four gospels are the names of these books authors: Matthew, Mark, Luke, and John. These men recorded some of what Jesus said and did during His life and ministry, in order to present an accurate picture for you to know who Jesus is and why He came. They wrote down the words of His teaching, His interactions with others, His miracles for those in need, and His death and resurrection. They also show how Jesus' coming fulfilled the prophecies and promises of the Old Testament. The God of the Old and New Testaments is the same God.

Instructions for Your Outline

> Write **Gospels** in the top left section of your outline, next to Roman numeral one ("I"). Next to "Gospel" put an **equal sign (=)**, followed by **4 Books**. Above "Gospels" write, **(Good News)**.

The word **"gospel" means good news**. Each of the authors of the four gospels was selective in choosing what to write down about the things Jesus said and did. Their selection of sayings and events from Jesus' life and ministry give us a clear picture of who Jesus is and why He came. As you read the gospel accounts, you will see that Jesus is the Jewish Messiah who fulfilled the Old Testament prophecies: He is the Savior of the world and He is the Son of God, the Lord of all creation! When you understand who Jesus is and why He came, you know the good news: Jesus is God's Son who came to save you from your sins.

When you understand who Jesus is and why He came, you know the good news: Jesus is God's Son who came to save you from your sins.

New Testament Books

(Good News)
I. *Gospels = 4 Books*

Matthew = tax collector, apostle
- *wise men follow star (2)*
- *Sermon on the mount (5-7)*

Mark = young man

Luke = physician
- *shepherds at the stable (2)*
- *Parables: Good Samaritan (10), Rich Fool (12), Prodigal Son (15), Lazarus & Rich man (16)*

John = fisherman, apostle
- *7 "I am" sayings (6:48; 8:12; 10:9,11; 11:25; 14:6; 15:5; 8:58)*
- *7 miracles*
- *Key verses 3:3; 3:16; 14:6; 20:28; 20:31*

Read what Jesus said & did
→ *Understand who He is & why He came* → *Good News!!*

II.

III.

IV.

New Testament Books

I.

II.

III.

IV.

Matthew = Tax Collector, Apostle

> Underneath "Gospels" write the name of the first book, **Matthew**, followed by an **equal sign (=)** and **tax collector, apostle**. Underneath "Matthew" write the following: **-- wise men follow star (2)**. And write on the next line: **Sermon on the Mount (5-7)**.

A disciple is a person who trusts in Jesus and is willing to follow Jesus in obedience.

Matthew is the name of the author who wrote this gospel account. Before he met Jesus, Matthew (also called Levi) was a tax collector. For several reasons tax collectors did not have good reputations among the Jews. To begin with, the taxes they collected were for the oppressive and foreign Roman emperor. The Roman soldiers, who ruled with an iron fist, were thought of as "intruders" by the Jews in the land of Israel. Their taxes paid for the Romans' oppressive presence. Therefore, tax collectors were considered to be traitors and were hated by their Jewish brethren. The amount of taxes collected was determined by the tax collector and most tax collectors were corrupt and rich because they collected much more tax money than what their Roman masters demanded. In the Bible you will find tax collectors grouped with "sinners."

But Matthew quit being a tax collector to become a disciple of Jesus. A **disciple** is a person who trusts in Jesus and is willing to follow Jesus in obedience. From among His many followers (or disciples) Jesus chose twelve men to be His "**apostles**." The word apostle means to be a "sent one;" someone sent on a mission. Jesus had a mission in mind for the twelve apostles. These twelve men walked with Jesus from the beginning to the end of His ministry. Their selection by Jesus and the training they received from Him was the basis for their authority and leadership role in the church after Jesus ascended to heaven. Matthew was one of the twelve **apostles**.

From among His many followers (or disciples) Jesus chose twelve men to be His "apostles." The word apostle means to be a "sent one;" someone on a mission. Jesus had a mission in mind for the twelve apostles.

Only Matthew, in **chapter 2** of his gospel, writes down the story of the **wise men who followed a star** to bring gifts to the newborn king, Jesus. In **chapters 5-7**, Matthew recorded a sampling of Jesus' teaching, which we call the **Sermon on the Mount**. In this sermon you will find the "beatitudes," which is Latin for "blessed" (5:3-10); the Lord's Prayer (Our Father) (6:9-13); and the Golden Rule (7:12). You read these chapters in your last reading assignment.)

Mark = Young Man

> On the next line of your outline write the name of the second gospel, **Mark**, followed by an **equal sign (=)** and **young man**.

Mark did not witness all of the events about which he writes. However, his relationship with the apostle Peter was so close that Peter calls him "my son" (1 Peter 5:13). Bible scholars believe that Peter is the eyewitness source to the events in Jesus' life which Mark writes down in his gospel. But for now, all you will need to remember about Mark is that he was a **young man**.

No one knows which gospel account was written first. Some think that the gospels are placed in the Bible in the order in which they were written: Matthew, Mark, Luke, and John. Others think Mark was written first. Of the four gospels, Matthew, Mark, and Luke are, in many ways, very similar to each other. These three gospels follow the same timeline of events in Jesus' life which the gospel authors chose to set down in writing. Many of the events written down in Matthew's gospel are also found in Mark and Luke's gospels. For this reason these gospels are grouped together and called the **"synoptic gospels,"** which means to "see together." To show the connection these three gospels share you can make a **bracket** in the left margin to include Matthew, Mark, and Luke. In contrast, John's gospel feels more theological than chronological in the way he structured his gospel account.

Matthew, Mark, and Luke are very similar to each other. For this reason they are called the "Synoptic Gospels," which means to see together.

Luke = Physician

> On the next line of your outline write the name of the third book, **Luke**, followed by an **equal sign (=)** and **physician**. Underneath "Luke" write the following: -- **shepherds at the stable (2)**. Underneath this write, -- **Parables: Good Samaritan (10), Rich Fool (12), Prodigal Son (15), Lazarus & Rich man (16)**.

The author of the third gospel is **Luke**, who was an educated man, being a **physician**. Like Mark, Luke was not an eyewitness of the events he recorded. However, he was very careful in the way he gathered information about Jesus from eyewitnesses who knew Him (Luke 1:1-4). Luke is also the author of Acts.

Only Matthew and Luke recorded the details of Jesus' birth. And only in Luke do we read about the **angels who appeared to the shepherds, who saw the baby Jesus in the manger.** (A manger is a feeding trough for animals.) This is written down in **chapter two (2)**, which was also part of your most recent reading assignment. It is only in Luke's gospel where we find some of Jesus' most famous parables: **The Good Samaritan (10:25-37), The Rich Fool (12:13-21), The Prodigal Son (15:11-32),** and **Lazarus & the Rich man (16:19-31)**.

John = Fisherman, Apostle

> On the next line of your outline write the name of the fourth book, **John**, followed by an **equal sign (=)** and **fisherman, apostle**. Underneath "John" write the following words: **7 "I am" sayings**. And below that write (small enough to fit on one line): **(6:48; 8:12; 10:9,11; 11:25; 14:6; 15:5; 8:58)**. Underneath this write, **7 miracles**. Add one more line under this and write, **Key verses: 3:3; 3:16; 14:6; 20:28; 20:31**.

John was a **fisherman** when Jesus called him to follow as a disciple. Not only was he one of the twelve chosen by Jesus to be an **apostle**, he was also, along with Peter and his own brother James, part of Jesus' inner circle among the twelve. John's close relationship with Jesus allowed him to witness Jesus' life and ministry from the very beginning.

John's style of writing is different from the other three gospel writers. John wrote about several encounters Jesus had with individuals, including the dialogue He had with them. An indication of the theological design of his book is his use of the number "seven." As you read his gospel you will come across seven **"I am sayings"** by Jesus, indicated by the chapters and verses you wrote: **6:48; 8:12; 10:9,11; 11:25; 14:6; 15:5.** (I am: the bread of life, the light of the world, the door, the Good Shepherd, the resurrection, the way-truth-life, the vine.) Of great significance is the time when Jesus referred to Himself with the words "I am" **(8:58)**. This is essentially the meaning of the Hebrew name for God (Yahweh), as when God revealed his name to Moses at the burning bush by saying, "I am who I am" (Ex 3:14). God is the ever existing one. When Jesus took that designation for Himself, He was clearly claiming His own deity.

John's gospel is very helpful in explaining how sinners can receive eternal life by believing in Jesus.

And whereas the other gospel writers record several miracles which Jesus did, John selected just **seven miracles**, which he called signs. The seven miracles he chose clearly present Jesus as the Savior of the world.

John's gospel is very helpful in explaining how sinners can receive eternal life by believing in Jesus. The **key verses** are examples of this. In chapter three, the reader is introduced to the meaning of being born again **(3:3)**. Jesus was referring to a spiritual birth that occurs supernaturally by the power of the Holy Spirit. In chapter one, John explains that becoming a child of God is a right given to those who receive Jesus by faith (1:12). Believers become God's children by being born spiritually into God's family. This birth is not by a blood line, you cannot gain salvation by being born into a Jewish or Christian family; nor is it by power of human will, you cannot earn salvation through your own efforts to try to change your life for the better; nor is it by any human authority, no religious institution of men can grant salvation; rather this spiritual birth is by the power of God (1:13). The most famous Bible verse is found in chapter three which promises eternal life to anyone who believes in God's Son **(3:16)**. Do you remember reading these verses in your reading assignment?

Jesus made it clear that He offered the only way for a person to be saved from their sin **(14:6)**. He is the way, the truth, and the life; there is no other way to the Father apart from Him. And in the twentieth chapter John makes it clear that the disciples understood that Jesus was both man and God **(20:28)**. Thomas is remembered for his doubting. But when he saw Jesus alive after the resurrection, he knowingly called Jesus his Lord and God!

At the conclusion of his gospel John explains why he selected the miracles, sayings, and encounters that he did **(20:30-31)**. He admits that there was more that

Jesus did than what he included. But his selection was made in order to present Jesus clearly as the Christ (Messiah). And when the reader understands who Jesus truly is, he or she can trust in Jesus with their heart and life. And John offers the assurance that life is found in Jesus' name, eternal life! This promise continues to us today. Do you desire eternal life? It is available only through faith in the Lord Jesus Christ.

Good News!

> Begin another line in this section and write: **Read what Jesus said & did =>**. Underneath this write: **Understand who He is & why He came =>**. And underneath that write: **Good News!**

Each of the gospel writers wrote about the things that **Jesus said and did** so that we can **read** for ourselves today the teachings and miracles of Jesus Christ. Anyone who takes the time to read the historical record that is preserved in the gospels of Jesus' birth, ministry, miracles, teaching, death, and resurrection, **will gain understanding of who Jesus is and why He came.** He is the Son of God who came to save us from our sins! And that is the **Good News**!

Instructions for Review

The exercises on the next page will help you to remember the information you have just learned. You will say the names of the books out loud as you do each of the exercises. In the first exercise you will write out the names of the four gospels along with Acts in three lists. In the second exercise you will match words with their correct description. And in the third exercise you will write out the description for the given word.

Anyone who takes the time to read the historical record that is preserved in the gospels of Jesus' birth, ministry, miracles, teaching, death, and resurrection, will gain understanding of who Jesus is and why He came. He is the Son of God who came to save us from our sins. And that is the Good News!

New Testament Review

The Gospels & Acts

1. Write the following names in three columns: Matthew, Mark, Luke, John, Acts

   #1   #2   #3

   .

2. Match the words with the description:

   ___ Gospel   A. A physician who also wrote Acts.

   ___ Disciple   B. A fisherman who became an apostle of Jesus Christ.

   ___ Apostle   C. Refers to 12 men who were chosen by Christ.

   ___ Matthew   D. Records what 1st-Century Christianity was like.

   ___ Mark   E. Refers to a person who becomes a follower of Christ.

   ___ Luke   F. A young man who became a follower of Jesus.

   ___ John   G. Means "Good News"

   ___ Acts   H. A tax collector who answered Christ's call to follow Him.

3. Write the description for each of the words listed:

   Gospel:

   Disciple:

   Apostle:

   Matthew:

   Mark:

   Luke:

   John:

   Acts:

Reading Assignment

In your reading assignment for this chapter you will read about the last week of Jesus' ministry from the last three chapters of Matthew's gospel. There are also a few chapters from Acts that will highlight some of the major events in the early church. The thirteen chapters to read are: chapters 26-28 of Matthew, and chapters 1-2, 9-11, and 15-19 of Acts.

Matthew 26-28
Acts 1-2, 9-11, 15-19

Even though Jesus' ministry lasted a little over three years, each of the gospel authors writes in great detail about the final week of His life. In **Matthew's gospel**, the final week begins in chapter 21 with the description of Palm Sunday. In **chapter 26** Matthew shares his eyewitness account of Jesus' last supper with his disciples. It was during this supper that Jesus instituted the ordinance which today we observe in our churches with the communion service, or the "Lord's Supper." This last supper was a Passover meal, which will bring to mind your previous Old Testament reading in Exodus. The Passover supper celebrated in Exodus was a foretelling of salvation through the shed blood of Jesus Christ and His death on the cross. **Chapter 27** gives a description of Jesus' trial, crucifixion, and burial. And **chapter 28** tells of the resurrection of Jesus from the dead and the great commission He gave to His followers!

In the first two chapters of Acts, you will read about Jesus' ascension to heaven and the Day of Pentecost, when the Holy Spirit came upon all of the followers (disciples) of Jesus. This is recognized as the moment when the church was born. In **chapter 9** you will read about the conversion of Saul (whose name was changed to Paul, and who became an apostle of Jesus Christ). **Chapters 10-11** show how the gospel spread as Gentiles became followers of Christ. In **chapter 15** you will discover how the early church settled an issue that threatened to bring division between Jewish and Gentile Christians. In this chapter you will see who the church recognized as their leaders. And in **chapters 16-19** you will follow Paul's trail on his second missionary journey. These chapters will introduce you to the people and churches who received the epistles, which make up the next section of the New Testament. You should make an effort to remember Timothy, Philippi, Thessalonica, Corinth, and Ephesus.

When you have completed your assignments, we will pick up with the next section of the New Testament: Acts.

CHAPTER 10

Acts

The historical section of the New Testament, told in a narrative style, consists of the four gospels: Matthew, Mark, Luke, and John and also includes the book of Acts, which is the topic of this chapter. The full title of this book is "The Acts of the Apostles." As you will remember the apostles were the twelve men chosen by Jesus from among His followers (disciples). These twelve men were with Jesus from the beginning of His ministry. During the three years of Jesus' ministry, they personally witnessed Jesus' miracles and teaching. They spent intimate time with Jesus while sharing meals and receiving personal teaching from Him. Jesus trained and prepared them to be leaders of His church after His departure. The church recognized the apostles' authority and foundational role of leadership (Eph 2:19-22).

Luke is the author of the book of Acts, and is also the author of the gospel that bears his name.

Luke is the author of the book of Acts, and is also the author of the gospel that bears his name. When you read Luke 1:1-4 and Acts 1:1-3 you see that Luke addresses both books to "Theophilus." The translation of this Greek name Theophilus is "lover of God." Luke may have had a particular person in mind whose name was Theophilus. Or perhaps he wrote both books for the benefit of all people, who through reading would become believers in Jesus Christ and also lovers of God. Luke's gospel recorded what Jesus began to do and teach, while Acts chronicles what Jesus continued to do through the Holy Spirit working through the apostles and in His church.

The focus of this chapter will be on three themes that you will find as you read the Book of Acts. These three themes are: the gospel, the church, and the Holy Spirit.

Instructions for Your Outline

Write **Acts** in the top right section of your outline, next to Roman numeral two ("II"). Next to "Acts" put an **equal sign (=)**, followed by **1 Book**. Underneath "Acts," write, **(themes)**.

New Testament Books

(Good News)

I. Gospels = 4 Books

 Matthew = tax collector, apostle
   - *wise men follow star (2)*
   - *Sermon on the mount (5-7)*
 Mark = young man
 Luke = physician
   - *shepherds at the stable (2)*
   - *Parables: Good Samaritan (10), Rich Fool (12), Prodigal Son (15), Lazarus & Rich man (16)*
 John = fisherman, apostle
   - *7 "I am" sayings (6:48; 8:12; 10:9,11; 11:25; 14:6; 15:5; 8:58)*
   - *7 miracles*
   - *Key verses 3:3; 3:16; 14:6; 20:28; 20:31*

Read what Jesus said & did
 ➡ *Understand who He is & why He came* ➡ *Good News!!*

II. Acts = 1 Book
 (themes)
1. Gospel (Acts 1:8)   *Jerusalem* ➡ *Judea* ➡ *Samaria* ➡ *ends of earth*
   a) *What is the gospel message?*
   b) *To whom is the gospel to be told?*
   c) *What response does the gospel call for?*
2. The Church
   a) *How are churches started?*
   b) *What do churches do?*
   c) *What is a good/healthy church?*
3. The Holy Spirit
   a) *Who is the Holy Spirit?*
   b) *How important is the Holy Spirit?*
   c) *How is the Holy Spirit received?*

III.

IV.

New Testament Books

(Good News)
I. Gospels = 4 Books

Matthew = tax collector, apostle
- *wise men follow star (2)*
- *Sermon on the mount (5-7)*

Mark = young man

Luke = physician
- *shepherds at the stable (2)*
- *Parables: Good Samaritan (10),*
  Rich Fool (12), Prodigal Son (15),
  Lazarus & Rich man (16)

John = fisherman, apostle
- *7 "I am" sayings*
  (6:48; 8:12; 10:9,11; 11:25; 14:6; 15:5; 8:58)
- *7 miracles*
- *Key verses 3:3; 3:16; 14:6; 20:28;*
  20:31

Read what Jesus said & did
➡ *Understand who He is & why*
  He came ➡ *Good News!!*

II.

III.

IV.

The book of **Acts** gives the reader a glimpse of historical events in the early life of the church. Jesus Christ is the central person of human history. Our calendars pay tribute to Him by using the abbreviations "BC" (before Christ) and "AD" (Anno Domini – year of our Lord). The book of Acts begins with a record of Jesus' last interactions with His followers just before His ascension; and then chronicles the activities of His followers after His departure. These activities include proclaiming the gospel message He taught them along with the resulting growth of His church.

None of these activities would have been possible without the supernatural presence of the Holy Spirit. To give you familiarity with this invaluable book, we will discuss **three themes** that are intertwined through the book: **the gospel, the church**, and **the Holy Spirit**.

The Gospel

> Underneath "Acts" write **1. Gospel (Acts 1:8)**. Underneath "Gospel" write **Jerusalem => Judea => Samaria => ends of earth**. You may use the given outline as a guide.

*But you will receive power when the Holy Spirit has come upon you, and you will be my witnesses in Jerusalem and in all Judea and Samaria, and to the end of the earth. **(Acts 1:8 ESV)***

The **gospel** is the first theme for us to consider and **Acts 1:8** is a key verse in the book of Acts. By way of review, the word "gospel" means the good news about Jesus Christ. Before Jesus ascended He told His followers that in a short time the Holy Spirit would come upon them. The Holy Spirit's presence in them would enable them to testify on Jesus' behalf wherever they traveled. Jesus made it clear that the good news of his life, death, and resurrection should be proclaimed right where they were and should go out to the ends of the earth.

The book of Acts records the movement of the good news of Jesus from Jerusalem to Rome, the capital of the Roman Empire. The spreading of this message required overcoming the barriers of ethnicity, language, religion, and culture. As you read Acts you will see that the gospel was never spread by coercion or force. It was always received voluntarily, and usually in the face of hostile opposition. In the early chapters of Acts we follow the gospel message from Jerusalem, where Jesus was crucified and resurrected, to the surrounding area of Judea (fellow Jews). A major barrier was crossed when Samaritans believed the gospel. But greater proof that the gospel is a universal message is shown by the reception of the Jewish Messiah by Gentiles! Jesus came to save all mankind, all who hear and believe the gospel.

The book of Acts gives the reader a glimpse of historical events in the early life of the church.

The book of Acts records the movement of the good news of Jesus from Jerusalem to Rome, the capital of the Roman Empire. The spreading of this message required overcoming barriers of ethnicity, language, religion, and culture.

> Returning to your outline, under "Jerusalem => ends of earth" write the following question: "**a) What is the gospel message?**" Underneath this write: "**b) To whom is the gospel to be told?**" And underneath this write: "**c) What response does the gospel call for?**"

These are three important questions that you will find answered as you read the book of Acts. **What is the gospel message?** Portions and summaries of several sermons written down in Acts inform us of what the apostles considered as the good news: Jesus is God's Son, who came to save us by dying for our sins. His resurrection from the dead is proof that He is the Savior. It is also proof that His death was accepted as payment for our sins. All who trust in Him will be saved! **To whom is the gospel to be told?** Everyone needs to be saved; therefore everyone needs to hear the good news of Jesus. People in every nation should be given the opportunity to know how they can be made right with God. **What response does the gospel call for?** The message of Jesus calls for repentance of sin and the acceptance by faith of Jesus as Savior and Lord. (See Appendix for: How can I be saved?)

The Church

> Now back to your outline, allow for a space between the first and second theme. For the second theme: write, **2. The Church**. Underneath "The Church" you will be writing three more questions. The first question to write is, **a) How are churches started?** The second question underneath this is, **b) What do churches do?** And the third question is **c) What is a good/healthy church?** All three of these questions about the church are answered in the book of Acts. In Acts, churches will find a pattern to follow for how to carry out their mission.

How are Churches Started?

Many students of the Bible place the time of the church's birth as the time of the Holy Spirit's coming as told in the second chapter of Acts. The first church was in Jerusalem where the first believers stayed following Christ's ascension. And like those first believers, the church today is made up of believers in Jesus Christ who assemble in His name to fulfill His mission of reaching the world with the gospel. **How are churches started?** In Acts we find that wherever the gospel was proclaimed, those who believed the message shared a commitment to assemble together in Jesus' name for mutual encouragement and shared ministry. Churches are started the same way today. Any group of believers in Jesus can commit to this same purpose. The first churches of the earliest Christians met in homes because they did not have church buildings. Buildings became possible in time after persecution eased up.

In Acts we find that wherever the gospel was proclaimed, those who believed the message shared a commitment to assemble together in Jesus' name for mutual encouragement and shared ministry. Churches are started the same way today.

What Do Churches Do?

The answer to this question is found in Acts 2:42-47. Under the leadership of the apostles, the members of the church were committed to being taught about the life of Jesus Christ and his gospel message, and were committed to fellowship with one another, which included breaking bread (perhaps a reference to the Lord's Supper) and prayer. They also cared for the needs of one another and were continually praising God and sharing their faith with others. The result was that the church was growing daily with more people being saved. Any church today that follows the example of the early church will have the same ministries of teaching (discipleship), fellowship (building relationships), worship, service, and outreach (evangelism).

What is a Good/Healthy Church?

The size of a church is not always an indication of its health. A better indication of a church's health is its maintaining of a balance of the ministries of biblical teaching, fellowship, worship, service, and gospel outreach. A church of any size that, with love and unity, carries out these ministries will be a church that experiences joy and healthy growth. Any person looking for a healthy, biblical church to join should look for these things: that the Bible is taught and people are hungry to learn what the Bible teaches, that you can see the love for one another in the congregation, that guests are welcomed in a friendly manner, that there are many opportunities to serve, and that there is an effort to reach the community and the world with the gospel.

The Holy Spirit

> There is one more theme of Acts to include in your outline. Write **3. The Holy Spirit**. Underneath this write three more questions in a list. The first question to write is, **a) Who is the Holy Spirit?** For the second question write, **b) How important is the Holy Spirit?** And finally, write, **c) How is the Holy Spirit received?**

Who is the Holy Spirit?

The Holy Spirit is a person, not a thing. The words of the apostle Peter in Acts 5:3-4 reveal that the Holy Spirit is a person (who can be lied to) and He is God. God reveals Himself in the Bible as a Trinity, in that He is one God, yet He consists of three Persons: Father, Son, and Holy Spirit. Even though this concept is difficult for us to comprehend with our limited understanding, it is a truth that is to be accepted by faith.

How Important is the Holy Spirit?

If you are consciously looking for the number of times that the Holy Spirit is mentioned in the book of Acts, you will conclude that the things that happened for the spread of the gospel and the growth of the church could not have taken place apart from the divine power of the Holy Spirit. The essential role of the Holy Spirit has led some to suggest that even though this book is called "The Acts of the Apostles," it could also be entitled "The Acts of the Holy Spirit." Even today it is impossible to truly live the Christian life or for the church to carry out its mission without the enablement of the Holy Spirit, who lives within the hearts of Jesus' followers.

How is the Holy Spirit Received?

In the book of Acts, the Holy Spirit only came to live within, or indwell, those who trusted in Jesus as their Savior. That is still true today. There is one difference between then and now. When the church began the Holy Spirit came upon believers only through the ministry of the apostles. This may have been God's way of establishing the foundational position of authority that belonged to the apostles. Since that has been established, believers now receive the Holy Spirit the moment they trust in Jesus as their Savior and Lord. (See Eph. 1:13-14)

In him you also, when you heard the word of truth, the gospel of your salvation, and believed in him, were sealed with the promised Holy Spirit, who is the guarantee of our inheritance until we acquire possession of it, to the praise of his glory. **(Eph. 1:13-14 ESV)**

Have you trusted in Jesus to save you from your sins? If not, what is hindering you from the most important decision of your life? We never know when will be our last opportunity. (In the Appendix you can learn what the Bible teaches about salvation: How To Be Saved. The topic of "salvation" will come up again in the last chapter.)

Instructions for Review

The exercises on the next pages will help you to remember the information you have studied. The questions are about the four Gospels, which we studied in the previous chapter, and the book of Acts. The first exercise can be skipped if you feel confident that you remember the names of all four Gospels. In the second exercise you will match names and terms with their correct description. And in the third exercise you will list the three major themes of Acts.

Any person looking for a healthy, biblical church to join should look for these things: that the Bible is taught and people are hungry to learn what the Bible teaches, that you can see the love for one another in the congregation, that guests are welcomed in a friendly manner, that there are many opportunities to serve, and that there is an effort to reach the community and the world with the gospel.

New Testament Review
The Gospels & Acts

1. Write the following names in three columns: Matthew, Mark, Luke, John, Acts

   #1   #2   #3

2. Match the words with the description:

   ____ Gospel   A. A physician who also wrote Acts.

   ____ Disciple   B. A fisherman who became an apostle of Jesus Christ.

   ____ Apostle   C. Refers to 12 men who were chosen by Christ.

   ____ Matthew   D. Records what 1st Century Christianity was like.

   ____ Mark   E. Refers to a person who becomes a follower of Christ.

   ____ Luke   F. A young man who became a follower of Jesus.

   ____ John   G. Means "Good News"

   ____ Acts   H. A tax collector who answered Christ's call to follow Him.

3. List three themes in the book of Acts:

   a)

   b)

   c)

Reading Assignment

Your reading assignment will introduce you to Scripture passages from the Epistles, which will be the subject of the next chapter. You are to read: chapters 1&2 of Galatians, chapters 1 thru 4 of Romans, chapters 1-4 of Philippians, chapter 1 of 1 Peter, and chapter 3 of 2 Peter. There are twelve chapters in all.

Galatians 1-2
Romans 1-4
Philippians 1-4
1 Peter 1
2 Peter 3

As you read **Galatians 1-2**, you will notice a serious tone to this letter written by the apostle Paul. You have read about his conversion to faith in Jesus Christ in Acts 9. Paul wrote to the churches of Galatia to address the problem of false teachers and their teaching within the church. In this letter he shares some personal background about the days of his early ministry. It is quite possible that the churches to whom he wrote were started during the first of Paul's three missionary journeys, which you can read about in Acts 13-14.

The **four chapters in Romans** present and explain the need for the gospel. Paul wrote this letter to the believers in Rome, believing that he would soon visit there if God willed it. Paul explains that all people, Gentiles and Jews are sinners, but anyone can be saved through faith in the Lord Jesus Christ. Paul then explains the difference between the two ways that people believe they can be made right with God. But only one way is God's way. Those who seek to be made right with God by keeping God's law will fail. But those who trust in Jesus are made right with God through faith, because of God's grace. It is the latter who obtain the righteousness of God, a righteousness that God gives! (See Rom. 3:20-26)

Paul wrote **Philippians** to a church which he began in Philippi of Macedonia, during his second missionary journey (Acts 16). He wrote this letter while under house arrest in Rome. As you read all four chapters you will notice the very positive tone of this letter, which is a surprise considering his circumstances. This epistle is a very encouraging letter to a church that was struggling with the threat of persecution and the influence of false teachers.

The apostle Peter wrote two of the letters that are in the New Testament. The **first chapter of 1 Peter** and the **last chapter of 2 Peter** are part of your reading assignment. A couple points of interest in 2 Peter 3 should be noted. Peter gives a description of the "day of the Lord," which is associated with the end of human history and the beginning of eternity, according to God's plan. Also, Peter recognizes and honors the fact that the letters that Paul writes to the various churches are Scripture.

The early church held both the Old Testament, and the writings which we now call the New Testament, in high esteem equally.

After you have completed your assignments, we will pick up with the next section of the New Testament: the Epistles.

CHAPTER 11

Epistles
or Letters

In the book of Acts we saw how the good news (gospel) of Jesus spread to both Jews and Gentiles, which led to the start of many churches. These new churches would have consisted of recent converts who were new in their faith in Jesus. The apostles were instrumental in both starting and establishing many of these churches. But even then, as is true now, no perfect church existed. Every church has its problems, weaknesses, and/or questions. Just as churches today face the challenge of living out the gospel in our cultural setting, so did churches in the first century, even with the presence of apostles. Without the complete Scriptures of the New Testament which we have today, the apostles' ministry was essential for keeping churches sound in teaching and in practice. The apostles were able to edify the churches by their teaching and leadership presence, and also by their letters (epistles), when they could not be present. As these letters were recognized by the church to have been inspired by the Holy Spirit, they were preserved and shared with other churches. In this way they became accepted as Scripture (See 2 Pet 3:15-16).

In this chapter we will survey the epistles (letters) of the New Testament. (An epistle is a letter; therefore we will use both words synonymously.) Most of the epistles were written by the Apostle Paul to churches which he personally planted. The book of Acts reveals the circumstances and difficulties Paul faced while planting these churches, which provides background information about these churches. Some of his letters were written to people he had trained for ministry and who needed wise counsel to overcome the problems they faced and encouragement to continue on with their pastoral ministries. The rest of the epistles were written by other apostles or by people who were recognized by the apostles. The destination of these letters is not always stated, which is an indication of their universal appeal to all believers in Christ.

In our study we will learn about all of the 21 epistles. When our study is finished you be able to name them in order. We will divide the epistles into two groups: **Paul's Letters** and the **General Letters**.

Just as churches today face the challenge of living out the gospel in our cultural setting, so did churches in the first century, even with the presence of apostles.

New Testament Books

(Good News)
I. Gospels = 4 Books

Matthew = tax collector, apostle
- *wise men follow star (2)*
- *Sermon on the mount (5-7)*

Mark = young man

Luke = physician
- *shepherds at the stable (2)*
- *Parables: Good Samaritan (10), Rich Fool (12), Prodigal Son (15), Lazarus & Rich man (16)*

John = fisherman, apostle
- *7 "I am" sayings (6:48; 8:12; 10:9,11; 11:25; 14:6; 15:5; 8:58)*
- *7 miracles*
- *Key verses 3:3; 3:16; 14:6; 20:28; 20:31*

Read what Jesus said & did
➡ *Understand who He is & why He came* ➡ *Good News!!*

II. Acts = 1 Book

(themes)
1. *Gospel (Acts 1:8) Jerusalem ➡ Judea ➡ Samaria ➡ ends of earth*
   a) *What is the gospel message?*
   b) *To whom is the gospel to be told?*
   c) *What response does the gospel call for?*
2. *The Church*
   a) *How are churches started?*
   b) *What do churches do?*
   c) *What is a good/healthy church?*
3. *The Holy Spirit*
   a) *Who is the Holy Spirit?*
   b) *How important is the Holy Spirit?*
   c) *How is the Holy Spirit received?*

III. Epistles (Letters) = 21 Books

A. *Paul's Letters*
1. *Romans*
2. *1 Corinthians*
3. *2 Corinthians*
4. *Galatians* ⎱ *Go*
5. *Ephesians* ⎰ *Eat*
6. *Philippians* ⎱ *Pop-*
7. *Colossians* ⎰ *corn*
8. *I Thessalonians*
9. *2 Thessalonians*
10. *1 Timothy* ⎱
11. *2 Timothy* ⎰ *Pastoral Epistles*
12. *Titus*
13. *Philemon*

5 T's {8–12}

B. *General Letters*
1. *Hebrews*
2. *James*
3. *1 Peter*
4. *2 Peter*
5. *1 John*
6. *2 John*
7. *3 John*
8. *Jude*

IV.

New Testament Books

(Good News)

I. Gospels = 4 Books

Matthew = tax collector, apostle
- wise men follow star (2)
- Sermon on the mount (5-7)

Mark = young man

Luke = physician
- shepherds at the stable (2)
- Parables: Good Samaritan (10), Rich Fool (12), Prodigal Son (15), Lazarus & Rich man (16)

John = fisherman, apostle
- 7 "I am" sayings (6:48; 8:12; 10:9,11; 11:25; 14:6; 15:5; 8:58)
- 7 miracles
- Key verses 3:3; 3:16; 14:6; 20:28; 20:31

Read what Jesus said & did
➡ *Understand who He is & why He came* ➡ *Good News!!*

II. Acts = 1 Book

(themes)

1. Gospel (Acts 1:8) Jerusalem ➡ Judea ➡ Samaria ➡ ends of earth
   a) What is the gospel message?
   b) To whom is the gospel to be told?
   c) What response does the gospel call for?

2. The Church
   a) How are churches started?
   b) What do churches do?
   c) What is a good/healthy church?

3. The Holy Spirit
   a) Who is the Holy Spirit?
   b) How important is the Holy Spirit?
   c) How is the Holy Spirit received?

III.

IV.

Instructions for Your Outline

> Write **Epistles (Letters)** in the bottom left section of your outline, next to Roman numeral three ("III"). Next to "Epistle (Letters)" put an **equal sign (=)**, followed by **21 Books**. Your outline will divide the Epistles into two groups: Paul's Letters and General Letters.

Paul's Letters

> Under "Epistles (Letters)" write, **A. Paul's Letters**. And underline "Paul's Letters." Under "Paul's Letters" write the numbers **1 through 13** in a list, being careful to leave room at the bottom of this section for the General Letters. (Use the model provided as a guide.) Next to each number, list the following epistles: **(1) Romans, (2) 1 Corinthians, (3) 2 Corinthians, (4) Galatians, (5) Ephesians, (6) Philippians, (7) Colossians, (8) 1 Thessalonians, (9) 2 Thessalonians, (10) 1 Timothy, (11) 2 Timothy, (12) Titus, (13) Philemon**. These thirteen epistles were written by the apostle Paul. Our goal is to help you remember the order of these books and to be familiar with them.

The "Romans Road" is a name given to a selection of verses which explain how a sinner can be saved and become right with God. These verses are: Romans 3:23; 6:23; 5:8; 10:9-10; and 10:13.

Romans, 1 Corinthians, 2 Corinthians

The first three of Paul's epistles are longest in content. Your reading assignment included the first four chapters of **Romans**. Paul wrote this letter to believers in Rome whom he hoped to visit soon in order to help them better understand the gospel. Romans gives a clear and logical explanation of the gospel of Christ, the message which was preached by the apostles. Even today many Christians find this epistle helpful in the sharing of the good news with others. The "Romans Road" is a name given to a selection of verses which explain how a sinner can be saved and become right with God. These verses are: Romans 3:23; 6:23; 5:8; 10:9-10; and 10:13.

Next are two of the letters Paul wrote to the church in Corinth, which we call 1 Corinthians and 2 Corinthians. In **1 Corinthians**, Paul addressed issues and answered questions with which this church was struggling. Many people find great comfort in what Paul wrote about love in chapter 13 and the resurrection in chapter 15. One of Paul's most personal letters is **2 Corinthians**, in which he opened his heart about ministry to address conflict that was aimed at him. His instructions about giving in chapters 8 and 9 are worth reading.

Galatians, Ephesians, Philippians, Colossians

On your outline, make a **bracket ("}")** on the right side to include the four epistles: Galatians, Ephesians, Philippians, and Colossians. There is a memory aid that will help us to easily remember these four epistles. Just remember "Go Eat Pop-Corn." To the right of the bracket, write, **Go Eat Pop-Corn**. **Underline the first letter** in each of these words to show that the first letter corresponds to each of the four epistles in their correct order: <u>G</u>alatians, <u>E</u>phesians, <u>P</u>hilippians, and <u>C</u>olossians.

Paul wrote **Galatians** to churches in Galatia, which today is in present day Turkey. These churches were probably planted by Paul during his first missionary journey (Acts 13-14). Paul sternly warns these churches against departing from the simple message of the gospel. In your reading of the first two chapters of Galatians, I hope you picked up on Paul's stern tone. And I hope you enjoyed reading about the early experience of Paul's calling and ministry.

Ephesians, Philippians, and **Colossians** were written by Paul while he was under house arrest in Rome. These letters were addressed to the churches in the cities of Ephesus, Philippi, and Colossae. Many of Paul's letters focus first on teaching doctrine, and then his focus shifts to practical application of that doctrine. This is true of **Ephesians and Colossians**, both of which share similar topics. By now you have read all four chapters of **Philippians**. Even though Paul was a prisoner when he wrote to the believers in Philippi, his letter to them is full of encouragement to a church which was experiencing persecution.

1 Thessalonians & 2 Thessalonians

Paul went to the city of Thessalonica in Macedonia, which today is modern Greece, to preach the good news of Jesus. Many of the people of Thessalonica placed their faith in Jesus Christ after hearing Paul preach and a church started there (Acts 17:1-9). But many others there were hostile to Paul and their threats against him forced him to leave before his ministry to the Thessalonians was completed. The epistles we call **1 Thessalonians** and **2 Thessalonians** are letters Paul wrote to a new church to encourage their faith and commitment to Jesus Christ.

1 Timothy, 2 Timothy, Titus

On your outline make a **bracket ("}")** on the right side to include 1 Timothy, 2 Timothy, and Titus. To the right of the bracket write, **Pastoral Epistles**.

Timothy and **Titus** were men trained by Paul for church leadership. The word "**pastor**" means shepherd. Timothy and Titus shared in the pastoral care of the churches started by Paul. Both of these men traveled with Paul and learned from him by serving with him. Paul sent Timothy to minister in the city of Ephesus; and he sent Titus to minister on the island of Crete. The New Testament includes two letters written to Timothy and one written to Titus. These epistles give encouragement and instruction on how to shepherd churches by feeding them the truth of the gospel and guiding them away from error.

Make another **bracket ("}")** on the left side to include 1 Thessalonians, 2 Thessalonians, 1 Timothy, 2 Timothy, and Titus. To the left of this bracket write, **5 T's**. This is our memory aid for remembering these five epistles which all begin with the letter "T."

Philemon

As we look at Paul's epistles you see we have briefly studied his letters to the Romans, 1&2 Corinthians, then Go Eat Pop-Corn (Galatians, Ephesians, Philippians, Colossians), and then the 5 T's (1&2 Thessalonians, 1&2 Timothy, Titus). To those twelve we add Paul's thirteenth epistle which he wrote to his friend and brother in Christ, **Philemon**.

Philemon was a believer who knew Paul, and whose slave ran away. This runaway slave, Onesimus, ran into Paul in Rome. This encounter led to Onesimus becoming a follower of Christ. Paul sent him back to Philemon with this epistle. In this personal letter, Paul encouraged Philemon to forgive Onesimus and to welcome him back, not as a slave, but as a brother. Christian love has led to the abolishing of slavery everywhere the gospel has been understood!

General Letters

Under Philemon, write, **B. General Letters**. And **underline "General Letters."** Under "General Letters" you will **make two columns of four, numbering from 1 to 8**. (Follow the model outline provided for your use.) In the first column write, **1. Hebrews, 2. James, 3. 1 Peter, 4. 2 Peter**. In the second column write, **5. 1 John, 6. 2 John, 7. 3 John, 8. Jude**.

These epistles carry the same weight of authority for Christian living as Paul's epistles. All of these epistles, like Paul's, were written under the inspiration of the Holy Spirit. With the exception of Hebrews, these general epistles bear the name of the author.

Hebrews

The book of **Hebrews** is an epistle that was written to Jewish Christians to encourage them to stay strong in their faith in Jesus. This book explains why the animal sacrifices and the kosher foods demanded by the law given by God to Moses no

The book of Hebrews explains why the animal sacrifices and the kosher foods demanded by the law given by God to Moses no longer apply to God's people. The reason for this change is that Jesus, God's Son and our High Priest, is the messenger and the mediator of the new covenant between God and His people.

longer applies to God's people. The reason for this change is that Jesus, God's Son and our High Priest, is the messenger and mediator of the new covenant between God and His people. The new covenant is far better than the old covenant, which was made obsolete by the death and resurrection of Jesus Christ. It is not known for certain who the author of Hebrews was; however, he was someone recognized as a leader by the early church.

James

The book of **James** is named after its author. Though he does not take credit for it, James was a brother of Jesus (See Mark 6:3). After Mary gave birth to Jesus, she and her husband Joseph had several other children (See Matthew 1:25). James and his brothers did not believe Jesus was the Messiah during Jesus' ministry. But after the resurrection, James became a believer and had a leadership role in the Jerusalem church as a leading pastor (Acts 15). He reveals the heart of a pastor in this practical epistle, which focuses on issues of spiritual maturity.

James had a leadership role in the Jerusalem church as a leading pastor.

1 Peter, 2 Peter

The apostle **Peter** had a prominent role in the gospels and in the first half of Acts. Two of his epistles have been preserved in our Bibles. Because Peter was a strong personality, his exhortation that calls for submission to God's will is powerful.

1 John, 2 John, 3 John

We have already introduced the apostle **John** as the author of the *Gospel of John*. John was also the author of these three short epistles and he was the author of the last book of the New Testament, the book of *Revelation*. As you can see, the distinction is made between his gospel and his epistles in that the epistles have a number preceding them: John (gospel), **1 John**, **2 John**, and **3 John** (epistles). John is known as the apostle of love because he encourages followers of Jesus to obey God's command to love one another.

John was the author of the Gospel of John, 1 John, 2 John, 3 John and Revelation.

Jude

Jude identified himself as the brother of James, which means that he was a brother of Jesus also. His epistle warns believers to be on guard against the deception of false teachers.

James and Jude were brothers of Jesus.

Instructions for Review

The following exercises will help you remember what you have just learned. It is to your benefit to say the names of the books out loud as you complete the first two exercises. Say both the names of the books provided and the ones you fill in.

The first and second exercises you will fill in the names of the missing epistles in four lists provided for you. The first exercise lists Paul's Epistles; the second lists the General Epistles. And in the third exercise you will match names with their correct description.

New Testament Review

Epistles (Letters)

1. Fill in what is missing: (Paul's Letters)

#1	#2	#3	#4
_____	Romans	_____	Romans
_____	1 Corinthians	_____	1 Corinthians
_____	2 Corinthians	_____	2 Corinthians
Galatians	_____	Galatians	_____
Ephesians	_____	Ephesians	_____
Philippians	_____	Philippians	_____
Colossians	_____	Colossians	_____
_____	1 Thessalonians	_____	1 Thessalonians
_____	2 Thessalonians	_____	2 Thessalonians
_____	1 Timothy	_____	1 Timothy
_____	2 Timothy	_____	2 Timothy
_____	Titus	_____	Titus
Philemon	_____	Philemon	_____

2. Fill in what is missing: (General Letters)

#1	#2	#3	#4
_____	Hebrews	_____	Hebrews
_____	James	_____	James
_____	1 Peter	_____	1 Peter
_____	2 Peter	_____	2 Peter
1 John	_____	1 John	_____
2 John	_____	2 John	_____
3 John	_____	3 John	_____
Jude	_____	Jude	_____

3. Match the name with its correct description:

____ Paul   A. He wrote a gospel, three epistles, and Revelation.

____ Hebrews B. He was a brother of Jesus, and became the pastor of Jerusalem.

____ James   C. He was a brother of Jesus and a brother of James.

____ Peter   D. Written to Jewish Christians.

____ Jude   E. He was prominent in the Gospels and Acts; two of his letters are in our Bible.

____ John   F. He was formerly a persecutor of Christians until Jesus appeared to him; after which he planted many churches. Thirteen of his letters are in our Bible.

Reading Assignment

Your reading assignment for this chapter will take you to the last book of the Bible: Revelation! Additionally some selected chapters from Hebrews will give you a flavor of this epistle, which teaches that Jesus Christ is the messenger and mediator of the new covenant! The twelve chapters to read are: chapters 1-2, and 8-9 of **Hebrews**, and chapters 1-6, and 19-20 of **Revelation**.

Hebrews 1-2, 8-9
Revelation 1-6, 19-20

In the **first two chapters of Hebrews**, you will read about the superiority of Jesus over the prophets and angels because the author presents Jesus, the Son of God, as the messenger of the New Covenant. This is why the salvation message spoken by Christ must not be neglected. In **chapters 8-9** the author refers to Jesus as our High Priest, who is the mediator of the New Covenant. Under the Old Covenant, the sacrifices of bulls and goats were offered continually. But under the New Covenant, Jesus offered Himself as a "once for all" sacrifice for sins! In God's plan the New Covenant has superseded the Old Covenant, which gives believers in Jesus confidence that their sins are forgiven, and gives them a clear conscience!

As you begin to read the book of **Revelation**, you will discover that its style of literature is different than any other book in the New Testament. Apocalyptic literature uses images and symbolism to communicate its message. And this makes it difficult for people reading this book for the first time to understand.

In **Chapter 1** John, the author of Revelation, explains where he was when he received the visions written in this book. In **chapters 2-3** you will read several brief letters from Jesus to seven churches in the Roman province of Asia, which today is the western most area of modern day Turkey. In **chapters 4-5** you will read John's description of his vision of heaven and the throne of God. The content of **chapter 6** is the breaking of the seals of the scroll, which includes the four horsemen. Do not try to figure out the meaning of each detail, but allow the images described to impress your heart with the reality that God is ruling over the events of the earth, even though His activity is hidden to the eyes of man. **Chapters 19-20** describe the return of Jesus Christ to the earth as the Lord of Lords, along with His final judgment! These chapters will familiarize you with some of the content of Revelation and its unique style of literature which will prepare you for the last book of the New Testament.

When you have completed your assignments, we will pick up with the last section of the New Testament: *Revelation*.

CHAPTER 12

Revelation

The full name of the New Testament's last book is *The Revelation of Jesus Christ*. This is usually shortened to just "Revelation." This final book of the Bible reveals the end of human history, just as the first book of the Bible, Genesis, is a record of the beginning of human history. The Bible claims to contain the true knowledge of where we came from and where we are going. Another name for this book is "the Apocalypse," which is Greek for "unveiling." The future completion of God's plan to redeem the world at the end of time is unveiled in this book.

The author of Revelation is the apostle John, who also wrote the gospel of John and the epistles of 1,2, and 3 John. John received visions from Jesus Christ while he was on the island of Patmos. The Roman Empire exiled John to this small island as punishment for his missionary activities. John was commanded to put into writing the things that Jesus revealed to him. Patmos sits off the coast of modern day Turkey, southwest of the city of Ephesus. It is believed that John ministered in Ephesus near the end of his life before he was banished by the Romans.

As you discovered in your reading assignment, the style of literature found in Revelation can be difficult to understand because of the imagery and symbolism in the visions John received. While depicting future events, the use of symbolism has the dual purpose of revealing some parts of the future while keeping other parts hidden. The Old Testament books of Daniel and Ezekiel, which are also prophetic in their writings, use this same apocalyptic style of literature. When you read Revelation you will be tempted to allow your curiosity to get the better of you by trying to figure out the details of John's vision of the future. Do not allow yourself to focus on the details. Instead focus on the bigger picture revealed by Revelation. God has a plan for the future. He is in control and His plan will unfold just as He intends. He has hidden the details, but His plan is very encouraging for those who trust Him!

As you read the Book of Revelation you will discover four themes that we will focus on in this chapter. Keep these four themes in mind as you read this book.

This final book of the Bible reveals the end of human history, just as the first book of the Bible, Genesis, is a record of the beginning of human history.

Another name for this book is "the Apocalypse," which is Greek for "unveiling." The future completion of God's plan to redeem the world at the end of time is unveiled in this book.

New Testament Books

I. Gospels = 4 Books
(Good News)

Matthew = tax collector, apostle
- wise men follow star (2)
- Sermon on the mount (5-7)

Mark = young man

Luke = physician
- shepherds at the stable (2)
- Parables: Good Samaritan (10), Rich Fool (12), Prodigal Son (15), Lazarus & Rich man (16)

John = fisherman, apostle
- 7 "I am" sayings (6:48; 8:12; 10:9,11; 11:25; 14:6; 15:5; 8:58)
- 7 miracles
- Key verses 3:3; 3:16; 14:6; 20:28; 20:31

Read what Jesus said & did
➡ Understand who He is & why He came ➡ Good News!!

II. Acts = 1 Book
(themes)

1. Gospel (Acts 1:8) Jerusalem ➡ Judea ➡ Samaria ➡ ends of earth
   a) What is the gospel message?
   b) To whom is the gospel to be told?
   c) What response does the gospel call for?
2. The Church
   a) How are churches started?
   b) What do churches do?
   c) What is a good/healthy church?
3. The Holy Spirit
   a) Who is the Holy Spirit?
   b) How important is the Holy Spirit?
   c) How is the Holy Spirit received?

III. Epistles (Letters) = 21 Books
A. Paul's Letters
1. Romans
2. 1 Corinthians
3. 2 Corinthians
4. Galatians ⎤
5. Ephesians ⎥ Go
6. Philippians ⎥ Eat
7. Colossians ⎦ Pop-corn
8. I Thessalonians ⎤
9. 2 Thessalonians ⎥
10. 1 Timothy ⎥ (5 T's)
11. 2 Timothy ⎦ Pastoral
12. Titus   Epistles
13. Philemon

B. General Letters
1. Hebrews   5. 1 John
2. James   6. 2 John
3. 1 Peter   7. 3 John
4. 2 Peter   8. Jude

IV. Revelation = 1 Book
(themes)

Future = how human history will end

Encouragement for believers = your faith will be rewarded! (on winning side!)

Reckoning & Judgment

Eternity = salvation complete
- damnation for God-haters (gospel-rejecters)

New Testament Books

I. Gospels = 4 Books

(Good News)

Matthew = tax collector, apostle
- wise men follow star (2)
- Sermon on the mount (5-7)

Mark = young man

Luke = physician
- shepherds at the stable (2)
- Parables: Good Samaritan (10), Rich Fool (12), Prodigal Son (15), Lazarus & Rich man (16)

John = fisherman, apostle
- 7 "I am" sayings (6:48; 8:12; 10:9,11; 11:25; 14:6; 15:5; 8:58)
- 7 miracles
- Key verses 3:3; 3:16; 14:6; 20:28; 20:31

Read what Jesus said & did
➡ Understand who He is & why He came ➡ Good News!!

II. Acts = 1 Book

(themes)

1. Gospel (Acts 1:8) Jerusalem ➡ Judea ➡ Samaria ➡ ends of earth
   a) What is the gospel message?
   b) To whom is the gospel to be told?
   c) What response does the gospel call for?
2. The Church
   a) How are churches started?
   b) What do churches do?
   c) What is a good/healthy church?
3. The Holy Spirit
   a) Who is the Holy Spirit?
   b) How important is the Holy Spirit?
   c) How is the Holy Spirit received?

III. Epistles (Letters) = 21 Books

A. <u>Paul's Letters</u>
   1. Romans
   2. 1 Corinthians
   3. 2 Corinthians
   4. Galatians   <u>Go</u>
   5. Ephesians   <u>Eat</u>
   6. Philippians   <u>Pop-</u>
   7. Colossians   <u>corn</u>
   8. I Thessalonians
   9. 2 Thessalonians   5
   10. 1 Timothy   T's
   11. 2 Timothy   Pastoral
   12. Titus   Epistles
   13. Philemon

B. <u>General Letters</u>
   1. Hebrews   5. 1 John
   2. James   6. 2 John
   3. 1 Peter   7. 3 John
   4. 2 Peter   8. Jude

IV.

Instructions for Your Outline

> Write **Revelation** in the bottom right section of your outline, next to Roman numeral four ("IV"). Next to "Revelation" put an **equal sign (=)**, followed by **1 Book**. Underneath "Revelation" write, **(themes)**.

Future

> Underneath "themes" write **Future = how human history will end**. (You may use the sample outline provided as a guide.)

The book of Revelation is prophetic in that it reveals the future, up to the end of time. In the first chapter, John is told:

> *Write the things which you have seen and the things which are, and the things which will take place after this.* ***(Rev 1:19)***

In the twenty-first chapter John wrote:

> *Now I saw a new heaven and a new earth, for the first heaven and the first earth had passed away. Also there was no more sea.* ***(Rev 21:1)***

Time began with the creation of the universe. The linear history of mankind and the earth will come to an end, an end which has already been determined by God. Because God is sovereign, He has the power to determine how the future will end. In His goodness He has chosen to reveal the outcome before it happens. The end of human history will mark the beginning of eternity. At the time of the end, God will make a new heaven and earth which will remain forever.

As you read Revelation, it becomes apparent that you are being given a glimpse of the **future**, a description of **how history will end**. This is a major theme of this book. God puts His reputation on the line when He reveals the future. But He does so to earn our trust. His track record of fulfillment is 100%! All of the Bible's fulfilled prophecy has happened as God said.

Encouragement

> Back to the outline, allow for a space between the first and second theme. For the second theme write, **Encouragement for believers = your faith will be rewarded! (on winning side!)**.

The book of Revelation has been an encouragement to followers of Christ in every generation, from the time of the apostles in the first century up to our present time. If this book is used only to satisfy one's curiosity about the future, there is a big risk of missing that encouragement. A clear theme of Revelation is that the **faith of believers will be rewarded!** Many Christians have lived through times of persecution, and many have died because of it. But the gates of hell cannot prevail against those who are united to Jesus Christ, the Lamb who occupies the throne of heaven! Christian believers are encouraged to overcome, **because they are on the winning side!** Jesus Christ is coming back as King of kings and Lord of lords. He will establish righteousness and will execute judgment on the earth. The names of all who trust in Him are written down in the Book of Life; and they will enjoy the fellowship of God forever!

In every generation, there have been times when evil has seemed to be in control, when oppression could not be stopped. All evil and oppression, and disease and death, will one day be destroyed forever, when Jesus returns! That is very encouraging for those who trust in Him!

Judgment

Another theme of Revelation to include in your outline is Judgment. Write **Reckoning & Judgment** under the previous theme.

Many have wondered how God can allow all the crime and injustice to happen on the earth. If He is truly righteous and just, why doesn't He do something about this? The answer is that God is already at work in the world, working in ways that we can't see, dealing with both sinners and saints. But there is coming a time when there will be a day of **reckoning** for all people who have lived. God will hold all men and women and all boys and girls accountable for their lives. All people, small and great, will have to give an account for how they lived. And all will be judged for their sins at the **final judgment of God**.

Sin is the disobedience of God's commands. Even though some people appear to get away with disobeying God, the reality is that no one escapes God's judgment. Revelation makes it clear that people, governments, nations, and rulers will be judged by God. The book gives a description of judgments poured out on the earth because of the rebellion of mankind against God and their refusal to repent. As your read Revelation, keep this theme of reckoning and judgment in mind.

Eternity

God has put in every heart the idea of eternity (Eccl. 3:11). Even though the human mind can't comprehend eternity, his heart yearns for it. It is not hard to imagine living forever. What is hard to imagine is ceasing to exist. Revelation teaches the reality of eternity, both for believers and for unbelievers. However, the experience of eternity will be quite different for those who believe the gospel and have placed their faith in Jesus to save them, than for those who have rejected Him.

Followers of Jesus Christ will experience the **completion of their salvation.** In our lifetime, we can experience salvation from sin through faith in Jesus. This experience includes the forgiveness of sin, the removal of guilt, and the hope of eternal life. But our salvation is not complete in this lifetime because of the presence of sin in our world and in our lives. But after the resurrection, salvation will be complete! Believers in Jesus will know what it is to be free from the power of sin, free from the punishment of sin, and free from the presence of sin, forever and ever! There will be no more sickness or death; there will be no more sorrow or tears. There will be uninterrupted fellowship with God forever. God will restore His creation of heaven and earth to what He intended.

In our lifetime, we have the opportunity to trust in Jesus for salvation from sin. But those who reject Jesus Christ by refusing His salvation will experience **damnation** (condemnation). Just as eternal life is forever for those who believe in Jesus; damnation is forever for those who **reject the gospel**, which is evidence of their **hatred of God**. God created hell for the devil. It is a place of torment that continues forever. All who join Satan in his hatred of God will join him in his place of torment.

There is only one way to avoid the judgment of God for our sins. Only Jesus can save you because He took your punishment for you when He died on the cross for your sins. If you sincerely repent of your sin and surrender your life to Him by faith, God will forgive you and cleanse you of all sin; and He will make you His child forever!

Consider the Following Verses:

And he brought them out and said, "Sirs, what must I do to be saved?" So they said, "Believe on the Lord Jesus Christ, and you will be saved, you and your household." (Acts 16:30-31 NKJV)

Nor is there salvation in any other, for there is no other name under heaven given among men by which we must be saved. (Acts 4:12 NKJV)

For God so loved the world that He gave His only begotten Son, that whoever believes in Him should not perish but have everlasting life. (John 3:16 NKJV)

Jesus said to him, "I am the way, the truth, and the life. No one comes to the Father except through Me." (John 14:6 NKJV)

For "whoever calls on the name of the LORD shall be saved." (Romans 10:13 NKJV)

Each of the themes found in Revelation, which you have written in your outline, are also consistently taught throughout the Bible. The future is in God's hand; He is directing human history to the end of the age. There is a reward awaiting those who put their faith in Jesus and who take God at His word; their hopes (expectations) will not be disappointed! There is also coming a day of reckoning when God will judge the world which He created. When this age ends, eternity will begin: salvation will be complete for those who love God, but damnation will come to God-haters.

Have you trusted in Jesus to save you from your sins? If not, what is stopping you from making the most important decision of your life? You never know when you will have your last opportunity. (For further guidance in your decision, see in the Appendix: How to Be Saved.)

Instructions for Review

The following exercises will help you remember the information you have studied and to help your memory. The questions are about both the Epistles (Letters), which were studied in the previous chapter, and the book of Revelation.

In the first exercise, say the names of each of the epistles in the list, both the names that you write and the names supplied. The first two lists are Paul's Letters and the second two lists are the General Letters. In the second exercise you will match names with their correct description. And finally, in the third exercise, you will list four themes of Revelation.

New Testament Review

Epistles & Revelation

1. Fill in what is missing:

Paul's Letters

#1	#2		**General Letters** #1	#2
_____	Romans		_____	Hebrews
_____	1 Corinthians		_____	James
_____	2 Corinthians		_____	1 Peter
				2 Peter

(Go Eat Pop-corn)

Galatians	_____		1 John	_____
Ephesians	_____		2 John	_____
Philippians	_____		3 John	_____
Colossians	_____		Jude	_____

(5 T's)

_____	1 Thessalonians
_____	2 Thessalonians
_____	1 Timothy
_____	2 Timothy
_____	Titus
Philemon	_____

2. Match the name with the description:

____ Paul   A. He wrote a gospel, three epistles, and Revelation.
____ Hebrews   B. He was a brother of Jesus, and became the pastor of Jerusalem.
____ James   C. He was a brother of Jesus and a brother of James.
____ Peter   D. Written to Jewish Christians.
____ Jude   E. He was prominent in the Gospels and Acts; two of his letters are in our Bible.
____ John   F. He was formerly a persecutor of Christians until Jesus appeared to him; after which he planted many churches. Thirteen of his letters are in our Bible.

3. List four themes in the book of Revelation:

a)

b)

c)

d)

Reading Assignment

Your last reading assignment will expose you to some of Jesus' most popular parables, which are found in the gospels. **Parables** are stories that teach and illustrate spiritual truth. Jesus was a master teacher! You are to read: chapters 10, 15-16 of Luke, chapter 4 of Mark, and chapters 24-25 of Matthew. There are just six chapters in all.

Luke 10,15-16
Mark 4
Matthew 24-25

In your reading of **Luke 10** you will encounter the Parable of the Good Samaritan. In this parable Jesus mentions a **priest** and a **Levite**. The "Abraham to Aaron Family Tree" in the appendix will remind you that Aaron, Moses' brother, was the first priest. Only Aaron and his sons, and their descendants, were chosen by God to be **priests**. Aaron and Moses belonged to the tribe of Levi. The rest of the tribe of Levi, known as the **Levites**, assisted the priests in the service of the temple. As you read ask yourself, what is the point of this parable? What does it teach you about the command to love your neighbor?

Luke 15 records three connected parables, but the most popular is the third, the Parable of the Prodigal Son. You could say that the message of the whole Bible is summed up in this parable. What do you think that message is? In **Luke 16** you will come upon two parables. This chapter was selected for you to become familiar with the Parable of the Rich Man and Lazarus. Who do you identify with in each of the parables you have read?

The parables in **Mark 4** demonstrate that the purpose of Jesus' parables was to enlighten to the hearts of His disciples to spiritual truth and, at the same time, leave His enemies in the dark. Only His disciples were given an explanation and interpretation of these parables, which revealed truth about the kingdom of God. Of particular importance is the first parable, the Parable of the Soils. If the seed is the word of God, and the soils represent various heart conditions, which soil represents your heart? Regarding the good news message of salvation through Jesus, does your response to this message reflect a "hard" heart, a "shallow" heart that shows enthusiasm until there is difficulty, a "crowded" heart which shows that other things are more important to you, or a "tender" heart that responds to the truth with trust, repentance, and surrender to Jesus Christ?

In **Matthew 24** Jesus gives His disciples a prophecy of events that happen after His resurrection and just before His return. His clear warning for His disciples is to be ready for His return because He is coming back. This is the context for the parables in **Matthew 25**. In this chapter each of the parables teaches that His disciples should live in light of Jesus' return. Are you ready for Jesus' promised return?

You can be ready, because God has provided you with a way of salvation, a way to be reconciled to God. Have you called upon the Lord Jesus to save you?

When you have completed your assignments, you can turn to the next chapter to learn how to use this book to help others become familiar with God's word.

Congratulations!

Epilogue

Congratulations! If you have completed all of the outlines, review sheets, and reading assignments, you are to be congratulated. I commend you for completing the study. It is my hope that you now understand why the Bible is the best-selling book of all time: it is the word of God! The question now is, where will you go from here? What will you do with what you have learned?

You are now familiar enough with God's word to begin reading it on your own! God had the Scriptures written and preserved for your sake. He wants you to read the Bible so that you may know Him in a personal way, and to know His will for your life. There is an inexhaustible depth to the knowledge of God and His wisdom that awaits you as you continue to read God's message of truth and love! I am hoping that this study has given you an appetite to read the word of God, the Holy Scriptures. The word "bible" means "book" in Greek. This is the book of all books.

The best way to read the Bible is to choose one of the books from the Old Testament or New Testament and to read through that book from beginning to end. Then I hope you will decide to read through the whole New Testament and the Old Testament as well. A book mark or a Bible reading schedule will help you keep track of your progress.

I would suggest that you begin with the New Testament. Some of the books in the Old Testament can be difficult for beginners to read. Difficulty can lead to discouragement, which can undermine your motivation to read God's word. However, even beginners can find interest in the history and poetry books of the Old Testament.

Everyone who reads the Bible will read passages that do not make sense at the time. Don't let that stop you from continuing. The more you read the Bible, the more you will understand. And if you make this a regular practice in your daily life, you will find spiritual food for your soul.

These verses from the Bible testify to the importance of reading and studying the Bible:

Jesus answered, "It is written: 'Man shall not live on bread alone, but on every word that comes from the mouth of God.'" (Matthew 4:4 NIV)

Therefore everyone who hears these words of mine and puts them into practice is like a wise man who built his house on the rock. (Matthew 7:24 NIV)

Heaven and earth will pass away, but my words will never pass away. (Matthew 24:35 NIV)

All Scripture is God-breathed and is useful for teaching, rebuking, correcting and training in righteousness, so that the servant of God may be thoroughly equipped for every good work. (2 Tim 3:16-17 NIV)

Leading a Bible Study

If this study has been beneficial to you, can I challenge you to pass on what you have learned to someone else? My purpose in writing this book was so that you could become familiar with the Bible and would be able to read it on your own. But I also intended that anyone who completed this study would be able to share this information with others. Let me remind you of what I wrote at the beginning of this book about how to use this book to help others.

Parents have used this study with their teenage sons and daughters. Adult children have enjoyed doing this study with their elderly parents. Because there are twelve chapters, this study fits well in a **Sunday School** class quarter (13 weeks). Review questions are supplied in the appendix for a review lesson as well. **Small groups** for adults in a church, or cell groups for teens within a church's Youth Group, all can also benefit from this study.

Another exciting opportunity for using this study has been with **neighbors** and **acquaintances**. Both church-attenders and non-church-attenders have found this study helpful and interesting. Many people have not been introduced to the Bible in a helpful way; some of these are often interested in learning more about the Bible when someone they know can introduce them in a non-threatening way. People from different denominations and faiths have found this study to be interesting and helpful. All it takes is an invitation!

The way in which I initiate Bible studies is by asking an acquaintance or friend if he has ever read the Bible before. Some people have, but many have not. Even people who consider themselves religious are not always familiar with the Bible. To people who are interested I explain that I have a study that can familiarize them with the whole Bible in a short time. I let them know that I would be willing to get together with them privately to do the study together. (I have met in homes, libraries, and restaurants.) Then I ask them, "Would be interested?"

If you ever have the experience of introducing someone to God's word, you will find it is a very satisfying one. I have often observed that once a person begins to read and understand the Bible it reveals an area of his or her life that they did not know exists! When you introduce someone to the Bible, you may find that you are introducing them to God. If this study has been a positive experience for you, be sure to include that in your invitation.

Missionaries who serve overseas can adapt this study into the languages of the people to whom they are ministering. The outlines that are employed in this book can be translated by the missionary into French, Spanish, Arabic, or any other language. The Bible is being translated in every language of mankind, and people in every nation are hungering for God's truth. But until people become familiar with the Bible, God's word will remain bread that is out of reach. But imagine what could happen when ordinary people have access to a simple tool like this study so that they can become familiar with the Bible? And then imagine the confidence they will have when they are able to introduce God's word to their families and friends!

It is my hope and prayer that God will use you to help scatter the seed of God's word, which will lead to the spiritual fruit of faith in the hearts of others!

Appendix

If you haven't already explored the appendix, here is what you will find in the pages that follow.

The Abraham–Aaron Family Tree shows the descendants of the Patriarchs of Israel. Abraham is the father of the Jewish people. The covenant God made with him was confirmed with his son, Isaac, and with Isaac's son, Jacob. Jacob's name was changed to Israel, from which the nation got its name. Jacob's twelve sons became the fathers of the twelve tribes of Israel.

The tribe of Levi is significant because Moses was descended from Levi, and because God chose Moses' brother, Aaron, for the priesthood in Israel. Only Aaron and his descendants were chosen for this special ministry. However, the rest of the tribe of Levi, known as the Levites, assisted the priests in the religious duties of sacrificing animals at the altar in the temple and in teaching God's law.

Also in the appendix is a study on **"How to Be Saved!"** that I hope will help anyone who is seeking the answer to this all important question. If you believe that the Bible is God's word, you are probably interested to know what God says about the way for you to be saved. The gospel is good news because it tells us, with no uncertainty, that Jesus came to save us from our sins. The study is based on Scripture so that your faith and confidence about eternal life can be based on the word of God.

In each chapter of this book you were given a reading assignment of various Bible passages that were examples of the contents of that chapter. All of the **Reading Assignments** for the whole study are listed in the appendix. There were times when I could not persuade a friend to meet together for a Bible study. But they were willing to read parts of the Bible and to meet me to talk about what they read. The Bible passages I suggested are the passages in the Reading Assignment list. As my friend's interest grew, I told them that I had a Bible study that would give them an overview of the whole Bible. I promised them that if they completed the study, they would be able to read the Bible and understand what they were reading. The study which I told them about is this book you are now reading!

Finally, you will find **Review Questions** for all three of the outlines you completed in this study: the OT Books, OT People, and NT Books. There are a couple of reasons for including these questions. First, you can test yourself to see what you remember! And second, these questions can be used by a Sunday school teacher as a review lesson.

Appendix

Abraham – Aaron Family Tree

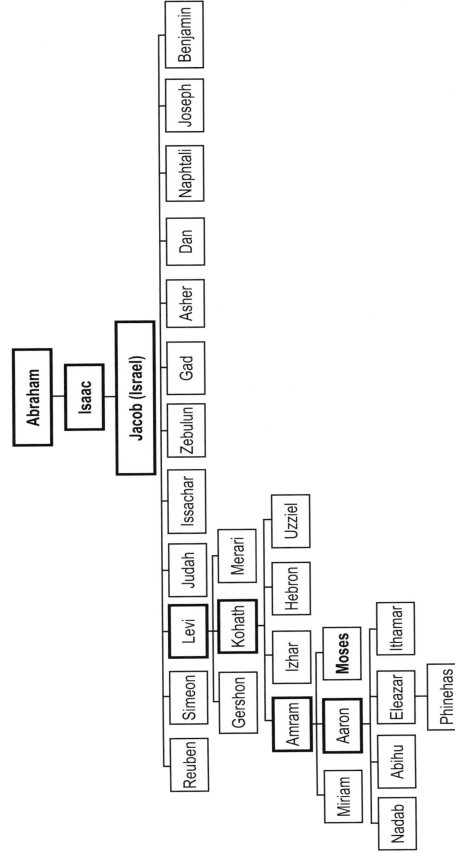

The *Abraham–Aaron Family Tree* shows the descendants of the Patriarchs of Israel. Abraham is the father of the Jewish people. The covenant God made with him was confirmed with his son, Isaac, and with Isaac's son, Jacob. Jacob's name was changed to Israel, from which the nation got its name. Jacob's twelve sons became the fathers of the twelve tribes of Israel.

The tribe of Levi is significant (outlined in bold boxes) because Moses was descended from Levi, and because God chose Moses' brother, Aaron, for the priesthood in Israel. Only Aaron and his descendants were chosen for this special ministry. However, the rest of the tribe of Levi, known as the Levites, assisted the priests in the religious duties of sacrificing animals at the altar in the temple and in teaching God's law.

How to Be Saved!

Is it really possible in this lifetime to know where you will spend eternal life after you die? The answer to this question is made very clear in the New Testament; that answer is yes! This is very good news! If you take the time to read further, you will find out that the Bible is clear in explaining what it means to be saved, how you can be saved, and know that you are saved. Because God loves you, He has made a way for you to be saved. If He wanted you to understand and have an assurance of salvation, you would expect Him to make it clear in the Bible. That is exactly what we see when we read the word of God, as the study below will show. (Locate the verse in your Bible in order to fill in the blanks with the missing key words.)

What Does It Mean to Be Saved?

The good news declared in the gospels is that Jesus came to save us from our sins! Consider the announcements by angels which were made around the time of Jesus' birth:

> *And she will bring forth a Son, and you shall call His name Jesus, for He will _____ His people from their sins. (Matt 1:21 NKJV)*

> *For there is born to you this day in the city of David a _____, who is Christ the Lord. (Luke 2:11 NKJV)*

The name Jesus means "Yahweh saves." Yahweh is the Hebrew name for God in the Old Testament, which is often translated into English as "LORD." Jesus is God the Son who came to save you. He became a man in order to do so.

> *Jesus said…"for the Son of Man has come to seek and to _____ the lost." (Luke 19:10 NKJV)*

Why Do I Need to Be Saved?

You can see from these verses that Jesus is the Savior and that He came to save you. Your salvation was the goal of Jesus' mission and the purpose of God's plan in sending His Son! Maybe you are wondering why you need to be saved. In fact, you will better understand what it means to be saved by first learning the reason for why you need to be saved. You need to be saved because of the problem of sin. You have sinned against God.

In regards to your spiritual predicament, it does not matter that other people have sinned worse than you. You are guilty before God because you have sinned. According to Scripture, everyone has sinned and no one can deny it. Sin is disobedience of God's commands. Your sin is a problem because it separates you from God, preventing you from being included in God's eternal kingdom. Your sin is also a problem because your guilt deserves God's punishment.

So that you can see for yourself what the Bible says about your problem of sin, let's look at some verses of Scripture.

The Problem of Sin

. . . for _____ have _____ and fall short of the glory of God, (Rom. 3:23 NKJV)

But your _____ have separated you from your God; and your _____ have hidden His face from you, so that He will not hear. (Isa. 59:2 NKJV)

Therefore no one will be declared righteous in God's sight by the works of the law; rather, through the law we become conscious of our sin. (Rom. 3:20 NIV)

When the Bible boldly claims that everyone has sinned, that includes you and me and everyone who has ever lived. Only Jesus lived a sinless life. Sin is a problem because it results in the spiritual corruption of our heart. Our sin makes us unfit for a relationship with God, who is holy. Some may try to justify themselves by pointing to the ways they are obeying God's law. But that very same law makes us aware of our sinfulness and of our falling short of God's glory.

Therefore, just as through _____ _____ sin entered the world, and death through sin, and thus death spread to all men, because all sinned. (Rom. 5:12 NKJV)

That one man by whom sin entered the world is Adam. (See Rom. 5:14)

You may wonder how we all became sinners. We were born with a corrupt heart, which gives us an inclination to sin. This inclination to sin is called "the flesh" or "sin nature." We inherited this sin nature from our parents, and our children inherit it from us. None of us needed anyone to teach us how to be selfish; that is inherent in our human nature. This inclination to sin goes all the way back to Adam and Eve's original sin of disobedience, which corrupted their hearts and made them sinners in God's sight. The sinfulness of the human race can be seen in the sinful actions, attitudes, thoughts, and words that hurts so many people in our world.

The Punishment of Sin

The reason why sinners feel distant from God is because our sin prevents us from having a relationship with Him. Sin separates us from God. Being holy, God cannot tolerate sin; He must and will judge sin.

> For the _____ of sin is _____ , but the gift of God is eternal life in Christ Jesus our Lord. (Rom. 6:23 NKJV)

> And as it is appointed for men to die once, but after this the _____ (Heb. 9:27 NKJV)

A wage is something that you earn; it is what you deserve. What you deserve for your sin against the eternal God is death. The consequence of death can be traced back to the sin of Adam and Eve. Death is a constant reminder to humans that sin has consequences. But there is more to death than just the physical death of our body. There is also the spiritual aspect of being separated from God. To die in your sins will result in being separated from God, who is the source of light and life, forever. No one who sins can escape God's judgment; and the consequences of God's judgment are eternal.

> Then Death and Hades were cast into the lake of fire. This is the second death. And anyone not found written in the Book of Life was cast into the lake of fire. (Rev. 20:14-15 NKJV)

These verses from the last book of the Bible refer to the "second death." After a person dies physically, there is a second death that is the result of God's judgment. The second death is an eternal separation from God. Because everyone sins, everyone needs to be saved. That includes you. But anyone whose name is in the Book of Life is saved from God's wrath. And everyone who trusts in Jesus has their name written in the Book of Life! That can include you!

Salvation is Through Jesus Only

> Now, brothers and sisters, I want to remind you of the gospel I preached to you, which you received and on which you have taken your stand. By this gospel you are _____ , if you hold firmly to the word I preached to you.

Otherwise, you have believed in vain. For what I received I passed on to you as of first importance: that Christ _____ _____ _____ _____ *according to the Scriptures, 4 that he was buried, that he was raised on the third day according to the Scriptures, (1 Cor. 15:1-4 NIV)*

There is a reason why I have left blanks in these verses for you to fill. That reason is to help you practice taking God at His word. These are not religious sayings that sound nice. These are the very words of God. As you understand the literal meaning of what the author of Scripture wrote as he was guided by the Holy Spirit, you will have a solid basis on which to place your faith. Your faith will be based on God's unchanging word.

You can see from what Paul wrote to the believers at Corinth that they had heard and believed the good news (gospel) of Jesus. It was the foundation on which their faith was standing. Because they were trusting in Jesus, having believed the truth of the gospel, they were saved! Jesus is the only one who can save us because He died for our sins. He paid the debt we owed; He took the punishment we deserved. No one else could qualify to do what Jesus did for you. This was according to God's plan which He foretold in the Old Testament Scriptures before Jesus was born.

For God so loved _____ _____ *that He gave His only begotten Son, that* _____ *believes in Him should not perish but have everlasting life. (John 3:16 NKJV)*

You can be saved from your sins if you also trust in Jesus who died for your sins. In the above verse, practice taking God at His word by putting your name in the blank spaces. God loves you. He gave His Son to die for you. He promises you eternal life if you genuinely trust in His Son.

The salvation that God promises is only through His Son. Through faith in Jesus: you are forgiven of all your sins (past, present, and future); you are made right with God (reconciled); you are cleansed and made holy in God's sight; you are adopted as a child of God; and you are promised an inheritance of eternal life! It is clear to see why the gospel is such good news!

You Can Know that You are Saved

It is common to question whether it is really possible to know that you are saved. But your faith must not stand on your feelings, which can change, but must stand on the unchanging word of God.

For by grace you have been _____ *through faith, and that not of yourselves; it is the* _____ *of God, not of works, lest anyone should boast. (Eph 2:8-9 NKJV)*

Do you see from what Paul wrote to the believers in Ephesus that they knew that they were saved? It was settled in their mind and heart because their faith was in Jesus, according to the truth of the gospel. Salvation is God's gift to everyone who trusts in Jesus to save them. If salvation could be obtained by works (or good deeds), people could boast about their salvation. But because of our sin, no one is qualified to boast.

> *For the wages of sin is death, but the _____ of God is*
> *_____ _____ in Christ Jesus our Lord. (Romans 6:23*
> *NKJV)*

A gift is not something that you earn. A true gift is something that is given freely. Love is the free gift of grace. Though we deserve God's wrath because of our sin, God in His love offers you the gift of eternal life (salvation) through Jesus, who died for you. Putting your trust in Jesus means to receive Him as your Lord and Savior.

> *I write these things to you who believe in the name of the Son of God that*
> *you may _____ that you have eternal life. (1 John 5:13 ESV)*

The apostle John states very clearly that if you sincerely put your trust in Jesus, you can know that you have eternal life! This is what God wants you to know before you die.

How to Be Saved: ABC

The way to be saved can be told in the simplest of terms that even a child can understand, but it is not simplistic. Let me use the analogy of a wedding. There is more to being married than just saying "I do." Certainly, getting married involves the formality of saying those words. But the essence of a marriage is a relationship built on love and trust. Similarly, there is more to being saved than just saying "I believe." The essence of being saved is that of entering a relationship with God that is built on love and trust. In explaining how you can be saved, keep in mind that this is not a magical formula. Rather, this is how you can express your repentance for your sin, your faith in Jesus to save you, and your desire for Jesus to be the Lord of your life. I will use the first letters of the alphabet in order to keep this simple: A-B-C.

A — Admit your sin to God.

Confessing your sin to God means to be honest with God. He already knows all about your sin. Instead of pretending that your sin is not that bad, agree with God that your sin is wicked. Let God know that there is no sin that you are not willing to give up. And ask God to have mercy on you and to forgive you for sinning against Him. He has already promised to forgive you and cleanse you of sin if you confess it with a sincere heart.

If we confess our sins, He is faithful and just to forgive us our sins and to cleanse us from all unrighteousness. (1 John 1:9 NKJV)

As you read 1 John 1:9, what does God expect you to do? And what does He promise that He will do if you do confess (admit) your sin?

B — Believe that Jesus died for your sins.

By now I hope that it is clear that you cannot save yourself. Jesus is God's only way for you to be saved. Trust that Jesus' death on the cross completely satisfied God's justice in punishing all of your sin. There is not a single thing more you can add to Jesus' sacrifice for you. Humbly accept God's gift of His Son.

And he brought them out and said, "Sirs, what must I do to be saved?" So they said, "Believe on the Lord Jesus Christ, and you will be saved, you and your household." (Acts 16:30-31 NKJV)

Paul and Silas were thrown in prison for preaching the gospel in the Macedonian city of Philippi. God used a great earthquake to shake open the doors of the prison and free everyone. The man in charge of the jail was about to end his life because he thought the prisoners had escaped. But Paul assured him that they were all still in the prison. That's when the jailer asked what he must do to be saved. What did Paul and Silas tell him? "Believe and be saved." And the apostle would tell you the same thing: Believe on the Lord Jesus Christ, and you will be saved.

C — Call upon the Lord to save you.

Every relationship requires communication. Prayer is how we communicate to God. Prayer is making a request to God that is in line with His will. If you have truly repented of your sin and sincerely believe that Jesus died for you, admit your sin to God and ask Him to save you because you believe that Jesus died on the cross to save you from the punishment for your sin. This is what it means to "call upon the Lord."

because, if you confess with your mouth that Jesus is Lord and believe in your heart that God raised him from the dead, you will be saved. For with the heart one <u>believes</u> and is justified, and with the mouth one <u>confesses</u> and is saved. (Romans 10:9-10 ESV)

For "<u>everyone</u> who <u>calls on the name of the Lord</u> will be <u>saved</u>." (Romans 10:13 ESV)

We have looked at the literal meaning of many Bible verses and have not taken those verses out of context. The meaning of the verses is clear and it has been explained how they affect your life. You are now able to make a decision which will determine the eternal destiny of your soul. You can pray and ask God to save you. Your relationship with God can begin with a simple prayer of faith. It is as simple as ABC! And God makes a promise to you that once you belong to Him, He will never forsake you!

When you pray, speak to God from your heart. Below is a model you can use to guide you in calling upon the Lord.

Dear God, I know that I have sinned against you. I admit that all of my sin is wicked in your eyes. I am amazed that you would choose to love me. And I thank you for Jesus who died for my sins. I don't want to continue my life the way I have been living. Please save me from my sins. I give my life to you, now and forever. Amen.

If you have prayed and asked God to save you, congratulations! Be sure to thank God for saving you! I rejoice with you! Making a choice to be a follower of Jesus is a decision you will never regret. It is also a choice that you should not keep secret. I encourage you to tell some of your closest friends. Let them know what Jesus has done for you! And when you are connected to His church, where His truth is taught and His love displayed, you will find encouragement and help for continuing to follow Jesus.

Reading Assignments

Old Testament Books

Law	Gen. 1-7; Ex. 19-20	(9 chapters)
History	Josh. 1-3; Judg. 6-7,13-14; 1 Sam. 16-18	(10 chapters)
Poetry	Job 1-3; Psa. 1,22-23; Prov. 10; Eccl. 3; Song 1	(9 chapters)
Prophecy	Isa. 9,53; Dan. 3,5,6; Jonah 1-4; (Ruth 1-4)	(13 chapters)

Old Testament People

Creation to Flood	Gen. 12, 21-22, 28-30, 37, 39-41	(10 chapters)
Patriarchs	Ex. 1-4, 7-8, 11-14	(10 chapters)
Nation of Israel	1 Kgs. 17-18; 2 Chron. 36; Esth. 1-4; Mal. 3-4	(9 chapters)
Kingdom of Israel	Acts 7; Luke 1-2; Matt. 1-2, 5-7; John 1-3	(11 chapters)

New Testament People

Gospels	Matt. 26-28; Acts 1-2, 9-11, 15-19	(13 chapters)
Acts	Gal. 1-2; Rom. 1-4; Phil. 1-4; 1 Pet. 1; 2 Pet 3	(12 chapters)
Epistles	Heb. 1-2, 8-9; Rev. 1-6, 19-20	(12 chapters)
Revelation	Luke 10, 15-16; Mark 4; Matt. 24-25	(6 chapters)

Review Questions
Old Testament Books

1. The OT can be divided into four sections; what are they?
2. What are the 5 books of the law?
3. What are the 5 books of Poetry?
4. What are the 5 books of the Major Prophets?
5. Who was the author of the first 5 books of the OT?
6. What book corresponds to the key word "Way Out"?
7. What book corresponds to the key word "Counted"?
8. He led Israel into the Promised Land after Moses.
9. Israel's leaders before they had kings.
10. She became David's great-grandmother.
11. The temple in Jerusalem was rebuilt after Captivity.
12. The walls of Jerusalem were rebuilt after Captivity.
13. How an orphaned Jewish girl became Queen of Persia.
14. A good man's faith persevered through really bad times.
15. Prayers & songs of praise.
16. Wise sayings on how to live wisely.
17. A man's search for satisfaction.
18. A song about marriage love.
19. He was a prophet who was thrown into a lion's den because he prayed to God.
20. He was a prophet who was swallowed by a large fish because he disobeyed God.

Review Questions
Old Testament People

1. The first one created, from whom we inherited our sin nature.

2. Adam's wife, "the mother of all the living."

3. He killed his brother Abel.

4. He was told to build an ark because of a coming flood.

5. A son of Noah and father of the Semitic people.

6. A descendant of Shem but who Jewish people refer to as father.

7. The oldest man who ever lived, 969 years old when he died.

8. The name we call Israel's forefathers.

9. A man known for his faith, God promised him a land and a son, and called him His friend.

10. Abraham's wife, who gave birth when she was 90 years old.

11. Abraham's long awaited son; his name means laughter.

12. He had 12 sons and his name was changed to Israel.

13. Jacob's twin brother, who gave up his inheritance for a pot of stew.

14. His brothers sold him out, but God turned it for good.

15. He led the Israelites out of Egypt after ten devastating plagues.

16. Moses' brother; he and his sons became the first priests.

17. He led the Israelites into the Promised Land after Moses died.

18. Israel's leaders before they had kings.

19. A remarried widow from Moab, King David's great-grandmother.

20. The strongest man in the world until his hair was cut.

21. Israel's first king.

22. Israel's second king, a man after God's heart.

23. Israel's third king, known for his wisdom.

24. Men of God who spoke the messages that God revealed to them.

25. The name of the Northern Kingdom after the civil war split.

26. The name of the Southern Kingdom after the civil war split.

Review Questions
New Testament Books

1. The NT can be divided into four sections; what are they?
2. What are the 4 books of the Gospels?
3. Who was the author of Acts and a gospel that bears his name?
4. Who was the author of Revelation and a gospel that bears his name?
5. Who wrote most of the epistles?
6. What are the first 3 books of Paul's epistles?
7. Refers to 12 men who were chosen by Christ.
8. What is a disciple?
9. What is an epistle?
10. This book is a record of what 1st Century Christianity was like.
11. What does the word gospel mean?
12. He was a brother of Jesus, and became the pastor of the church in Jerusalem.
13. This epistle was written to Jewish Christians.
14. He was formerly a persecutor of Christians until Jesus appeared to him; after which he planted churches. Thirteen of his letters are in our Bible.
15. He was a brother of Jesus and a brother of James.
16. He was prominent in the Gospels and Acts; two of his letters are in our Bible.
17. What are three themes found in Acts?
18. What are four themes found in Revelation?
19. Of Paul's epistles, which correspond to Go Eat Pop-Corn?
20. Of Paul's epistles, what are the 5 T's?

Index